フ⊃ 1976

5279763 HIBBS, J
          Omnibus

£2·50

Please renew/return this item by the last date shown.

So that your telephone call is charged at local rate,
please call the numbers as set out below:

	From Area codes 01923 or 0208:	From the rest of Herts:
Renewals:	01923 471373	01438 737373
Enquiries:	01923 471333	01438 737333
Minicom:	01923 471599	01438 737599

L32b

Hertfordshire
COUNTY COUNCIL
Community Information

0 2 MAR 2000

1 7 MAR 2007

8/12

L32a

L 33

THE OMNIBUS

THE OMNIBUS

Readings in the History of Road
Passenger Transport

edited by

JOHN HIBBS

DAVID & CHARLES : NEWTON ABBOT

Set in eleven on thirteen point Press Roman
and printed in Great Britain
by Redwood Press Limited Trowbridge and London
for David & Charles (Publishers) Limited
South Devon House Newton Abbot Devon

CONTENTS

List of Illustrations   7

Acknowledgements   8

Introduction   9

The Roaring Twenties
John M. Birch   11

Edinburgh Experimental Vehicles
Gavin A. Booth   34

**Bus Services on the Great North Road between Edinburgh
and Doncaster**
J. Graeme Bruce   54

My First Seventeen Years of Management
Norman H. Dean   81

Passenger Transport in Bristol in the Victorian Era
T.W.II. Gailey   104

Early Omnibus Services in Birmingham, 1834-1905
Alec G. Jenson   113

One Hundred Years of Railway-Associated Omnibus Services
Charles E. Lee   147

A Chapter in London Bus History
Charles E. Lee   181

Extended Tours by Motor Coach
E.L. Taylor   191

List of Omnibus Society Papers on Historical Subjects   205

...e Publishers regret that a line has been omitted from page 189
...e following should be inserted after line 20:

(out of 38,040) and 1,500 deferred 1s. (out of

...page 188, line 20, the date should read 1912, not 1913.

ILLUSTRATIONS

PLATES

	Page
An early GWR motor bus	Frontispiece
Edinburgh electric tram, 1933	49
Edinburgh motor bus, 1933	49
Edinburgh motor bus, 1961	49
Northern General bus station, Durham City	50
Hebble motor bus, 1947	50
Bristol horse tram, 1875	67
Bristol steam tram and trailer, 1881	67
Bristol electric tram and trailer	67
Birmingham steam tram and trailer	68
Birmingham horse buses, 1869	117
Birmingham horse bus, 1860	117
GWR motor bus, late 1920's	118
LNER motor bus, 1929	118
London General 'X' type motor bus	135
London General 'B' type motor bus	135
London General 'B' type motor bus	136

In text

'Family tree' of Birmingham omnibus operators	116
Train and Omnibus Time Table, Aberdeen to Strathdon	150-1

Maps

Darlington Triumph motor bus routes, 1950	64
Hebble motor bus routes, 1929	94
Hebble motor bus routes, 1939	95
Birmingham Tramway and Omnibus Routes, 1895	124
GNSR motor bus routes, 1912	159
GWR motor bus routes, 1929	160-1
GER motor bus routes, 1908	175

ACKNOWLEDGEMENTS

I have been able to make free use of the Omnibus Society's valuable collection of photographic blocks, many of which have been presented to the Society. The following are from this source: 49, 50 (above) (originally *Railway Gazette*), 68, 117, 118. 50 (below) is by courtesy of Mr Gavin Booth; photographs on page 67 are from the J.B. Appleby collection, by courtesy of the Bristol Omnibus Company Ltd; 135 and 136 are by courtesy of London Transport. The line drawing of *Darlington Triumph* routes is from a block in the Omnibus Society's collection. The frontispiece is by courtesy of British Rail Archives.

JOHN HIBBS

INTRODUCTION

In November 1969 the Omnibus Society held a dinner in London to celebrate its fortieth anniversary and to pay tribute to its founders and past presidents; so many distinguished guests were present that they could not all be accommodated at the top table. In the last of the papers included in this volume, Mr E.L. Taylor describes the Society as a unique institution, and the point is well illustrated by the number of senior managers of the motor bus industry who have accepted its presidency, with the consequent duty of contributing a serious paper to the Society's proceedings. At the same time, the ordinary members of the Society include both amateurs and professionals of transport, and the high standard of accuracy and enthusiasm that they display was remarked upon by several speakers at the anniversary dinner.

The Society's interests are not limited to the historical field, but in recording the development of the industry as well as in exploring its past, members have a special contribution to make to the study of transport history. It was my own indebtedness in preparing *The History of British Bus Services* that led me to suggest the publication of a number of papers that I had found of particular value, and that seemed to me to call for wider circulation. With the agreement of the Council of the Society, I have tried to select papers with a wide range of interest, whose value lies not only in their wealth of detail but also in the light that they shed on various phases in the evolution of buses and bus services. Their selection has not been an easy task, on account of the wealth of material available, but I have tried to use mainly papers that are no longer in print and at the same time to include something for a variety of interests, while preserving some geographical balance.

My thanks are due to the authors of the papers, all of whom have revised their contributions to bring them up to date, and several of whom have provided important new material. Mr Eric Axten has contributed maps and diagrams and Mr Gavin Booth, Editor of the Society's publications, has helped with the illustrations, many of which are taken from the Society's extensive collection. The copyright in all the papers included here remains with the Omnibus Society.

City of London Polytechnic   JOHN HIBBS

THE ROARING TWENTIES
John M. Birch

Mr Birch was President of the Omnibus Society in 1954, and in this Presidential Address he outlines the history of his family business during the era of the London 'pirates'. As this book goes to press, the announcement has been made that Birch Bros Ltd has disposed of its last regular bus services, but the company remains active in the London coaching trade, and Mr Birch is today its Deputy Chairman.

When Birch Bros Ltd abandoned the field of London omnibus operation in 1912 after sixty-five years, and after a most expensive experience with a fleet of motor buses in 1904-7, it was with the firm intention that the ancient foes, particularly Tillings, should not be left permanently in possession of the field. At the same time, the lesson had been well learnt that it was essential to possess motor engineering knowledge in order to run buses. Naturally neither my grandfather nor my father had such knowledge, but there appeared to be some promising material in the person of my brother, Raymond, and thus whilst still at school during the first world war, he spent his holidays in the workshops of various motor firms, thereafter taking a three year mechanical engineering course at University College, London, followed by practical experience with Leyland Motors Ltd and other companies. Raymond joined Birch Bros as engineer in August 1924, and in the following month the company ordered ten London omnibus type LB5 chassis from Leyland Motors Ltd and started to build 48-seater double-deck bodies in their own coachworks. At the same time, reconstruction was commenced on the Company's Kentish Town premises to make them suitable as an omnibus garage.

My grandfather was strongly of the opinion that before placing these omnibuses in service in competition with the London General Omnibus Company, the latter should first be approached to know whether they would be prepared, having regard to their previous co-ordinated working with the Birch family for a period of some sixty years, to enter into an agreement with Birch Bros by which the latter would operate ten omnibuses in association with the LGOC, working them in co-ordinated service upon one of the latter's existing routes, or if need be, upon some entirely new route. Accordingly, my grandfather called upon Mr Pick, who promised to lay the matter before the directors. He shortly after requested my grandfather and father to call at the offices of the Underground Group, when he informed them that his directors could not consider any such agreement. Birch Bros thereupon determined that they would operate their omnibuses in competition with the LGOC if need be, but that as far as possible any routes they opened would be such as would provide different and additional facilities to those already existing, and that wherever possible they would run their service in association and co-ordination with other proprietors, and this policy was consistently adhered to.

Meanwhile Birch Bros had been approached by the Overground undertaking, who wished Birch Bros to join them in associated operation of certain new routes between Potters Bar and Victoria, etc, and accordingly, on 26 September 1924, Birch Bros made application to the Commissioner of Police for approval of four new routes simultaneously with a similar application by the Overground Company. The routes were as follows:

(1) Potters Bar and Hampton Court
(2) Hadley Highstone and Elephant & Castle
(3) Muswell Hill and Victoria Station
(4) Potters Bar and Victoria Station

and on 6 October the Commissioner of Police approved these routes.

On 25 November the first Leyland chassis was delivered, and early in December Chief Constable Bassom convened a meeting at Scotland Yard of all omnibus proprietors to explain the new methods of licensing omnibuses, including the method of depositing schedules of times and fares, which were going to be brought into effect on 1 January 1925, in accordance with Section 6 of the London Traffic Act, 1924.

Towards the end of the month the second chassis was delivered, and the City Omnibus Co Ltd suggested that Birch Bros joined them in the operation of a new route between Highgate and Brockley via Oxford Circus and Victoria.

On 21 January 1925, the necessary schedules having been deposited the previous day, two double-deck Leyland Omnibuses were placed on Route 536, Highgate and Brockley Rise, in conjunction with the City Motor Omnibus Co Ltd and the United Motor Omnibus Co Ltd, the total number of omnibuses in service being twentyfive and the service interval six to seven minutes.

On 17 February the Minister published his intention of making the first 'Restricted Streets Order' (London Traffic Restricted Streets Order, 1925), stated to take effect retrospectively from 1 January 1925. This order was made under Section 7 of the London Traffic Act 1924, which gave powers to the Minister to limit the number of omnibuses plying on certain streets within the City of London and the Metropolitan Police District.

The first 'Restricted Streets Order' declared that on a very large number of streets, mostly busy main thoroughfares in the central area, no omnibuses would be permitted to ply for hire except those which had schedules deposited, and in force, on 1 January, and those which were in force on 21 January on Route 536 for two omnibuses, were declared retrospectively null and void.

A number of other proprietors were also affected by the retrospective nature of this order, and the independent proprietors, who were practically all members of the Association of London Omnibus Proprietors, protested very strongly against the unfairness of such a regulation. Their efforts to obtain relief met with considerable sympathy from Members of Parliament, and the Minister of Transport was asked a great many questions in the House of Commons relating to the hardships involved.

On 28 February, Birch Bros wrote to the chairman of the London Traffic Advisory Committee (upon whose advice the Minister had made the Order) protesting against the Order, and suggesting 1 July should be the effective date, thus enabling them to place in service all the omnibuses which they had ordered, of which only two had been completed at the date of the Order. The Minister replied, enclosing a form to be completed and returned to the Secretary of the Advisory Committee as a prelude to a hearing of the hard cases by that Committee.

On 12 March, in answering a question in the House of Commons, the Minister stated:

'There may be cases of real hardship and I understand the (Traffic Advisory) Committee are going into these cases and I hope they will be able to recommend the fullest sympathy it is possible to give to this class of people. I do not think there are a great number, but I will do everything in my power to avoid injustice to them.'

Accordingly, on 15 March, my father attended before a small sub-committee of the Advisory Committee and stated his case, which was, shortly, that Birch Bros had in all good faith ordered omnibus chassis some months before, had been unable to obtain an early delivery, and had consequently got five omnibuses on their hands as well as a garage reconstructed at considerable expense, none of which would be any use to them if the effective date of the Order stood at 1 January. He particularly objected to the retrospective nature of the ban.

On 18 March the Association of London Omnibus Proprietors circulated a statement in the House of Commons in support of an address for the Order to be annulled.

On 24 March three more omnibuses were licensed by the Police, but there was no route to put them on. Those on

Route 536, of course, continued to run pending the Minister's final decision as to the date of the Order, and on 7 April my father attended before the Traffic Advisory Committee to be told that nothing would be done to help Birch Bros in the matter, and that their omnibuses would have to come off Route 536.

Chief Constable Bassom, however, handed to my father a folio of multi-typed sheets headed 'Suggestions for Routes in Unrestricted Streets,' with the words, 'Here is a list of routes upon which you may work your omnibuses, and I would advise you to make up your mind quickly which route of them you will work, as there is another restriction order coming which will preclude further omnibuses being placed upon tram routes.' This list of routes included many recognisable as having been suggested by various independent proprietors in response to an inquiry from the ALOP to its members calling for such suggestions in case the first Restriction Order should be fully applied. Among them was one between Hadley Highstone and Wandsworth Bridge, via North Finchley, Hendon, Cricklewood, Willesden, Acton and Shepherds Bush, which was suggested by the Cornwall Omnibus Company.

Within a day or two representatives of a number of independent proprietors, including Cornwall and Birch Bros, met at the ALOP offices to discuss the provision of a service on this route. My father, owing to his long previous experience of association working, at once took the lead and proposed that an association be formed to operate a regular headway service. The other proprietors accepted the proposal and authorised my father to prepare a time list or running schedule.

The total omnibuses for the route were twentysix, of which Birch Bros were to provide five, two of these being withdrawn from Route 536; it was decided to operate the full route from Hadley Highstone on Sundays only and to run between North Finchley (Swan and Pyramids) and Wandsworth Bridge on Mondays to Saturdays. Police approval of the route was requested and obtained and operation commenced on 11 April 1925, as Route 526, with a regular headway of nine minutes. It had been obvious from the beginning that the route ought to pass through Golders Green and Childs Hill instead of Hendon and the Edgware Road, but it had been thought undesirable to ask for any modification of the route originally suggested owing to Mr Bassom's warning as to getting on the route quickly.

On 17 April, the Minister of Transport wrote to all omnibus proprietors, advising them of his intention to make a further Restricted Streets Order, including most tramway routes, and asking for representations before 1 May, to which Birch Bros replied requesting the exemption of Finchley Road and Cricklewood Lane in view of the desire of the 526 proprietors to divert their route away from Hendon and through Golders Green.

Soon after, as a result of application to the Commissioner of Police, Route 526 was re-defined and operated via Finchley Road and Cricklewood Lane as desired.

On 16 May the Minister wrote to Birch Bros and other proprietors on Routes 526 and 17, stating that he was considering what variation might be desirable in the frequency of omnibuses on restricted streets, either generally or in particular hours and requiring a census to be taken of the passengers on the section of Route 526 between Acton and Shepherds Bush.

On 18 May, as a result of previous arrangements, nearly all independent omnibus undertakings in London reduced their fares, including those of Route 526.

On 21 May a number of questions were asked in the House of Commons regarding the proprietors injured by the first Restricted Streets Order, and Sir Henry Jackson replied for the Minister that: 'All have been found new routes and are now satisfied. They are earning livelihoods on routes which apart from stabilisation would not have come into existence at all.'

On 5 June the Minister wrote to all proprietors, announcing that the second Restricted Streets Order was in force as from

3 June and that there would be a Public Inquiry at the Guildhall, Westminster, on 22 June.

During the next ten days Birch Bros and other affected proprietors, in response to a request from the ALOP, sent to both the ALOP and the Minister details of the injustices suffered by them under the first Restricted Streets Order.

On 18 June the Minister wrote to Birch Bros referring to the representations which had been made against the Restricted Streets Order and stated that upon the advice of the Traffic Advisory Committee he had decided to make Amending Regulations post-dating the first Restricted Streets Order from 1 January 1925, to 17 February 1925, and thus permitting Birch Bros to replace two omnibuses on Route 536. Birch Bros took advantage of this and accordingly recommenced operation on Route 536 on 1 August 1925.

Route 536 (Highgate and Brockley) was extended to Catford on 1 August 1925, and when it was further extended through Beckenham to Elmers End on 14 April 1927, the extension permitted Birch Bros to place an additional omnibus on the route without lessening the headway between the total number of vehicles as between Highgate and Catford.

On 1 August the Minister wrote to Birch Bros and other 526 proprietors, again stating he was considering what variations, if any, might be desirable in the frequency of omnibuses on Restricted Streets, either generally or in particular hours, and requiring a census of Route 526 between North Finchley and Horn Lane, Acton.

On 31 August the association of proprietors on Route 526 was given a formal title — The West London Association (WLA) — and a minute book was kept of the meetings.

During November a number of minor variations were obtained in the schedules of Route 526 in order to close the gaps in the service caused by buses which had left the route to return to their old routes in accordance with the Amendment Regulations of June, and also for the more convenient operation of the service, and these concessions were obtained from the Minister and the Police on Birch Bros' representation that a proper co-ordinated service was being provided, as in fact was the case. No dispensation or concession could be obtained, however, which would allow a small operator with one bus to borrow a spare bus from a large operator when his own vehicle was in dock or under overhaul, although this was obviously desirable.

In January 1926, the Minister announced his intention of seriously cutting down the number of omnibus services on a number of tramway routes, including Routes 17 and 526. On Route 17 the reduction was so serious that one proprietor, Beatty, operating eastward as far as Shepherds Bush only, was not to be allowed to operate at all, and the service on Route 526 was to be reduced from a nine-minute to a half-hour headway, that is to say, two-thirds of the buses would have to be withdrawn, or fourteen out of a total of twentyone, meaning a reduction for Birch Bros of from three to one, while at the same time, of course, the buses that did remain would have carried far fewer passengers per bus owing to the uselessness to the public of a half-hourly service. It was immediately realised by all the independents that just as the first Restriction Order had been the first blow, this was to be the Minister's second blow, again retrospective, and even more directly aimed at independent proprietors than the original attack.

Immense public indignation was aroused and the independent proprietors immediately set about obtaining signatures for a public petition to the House of Commons praying that no steps be taken to increase the difficulties of the travelling public.

On 6 March the Minister wrote to Birch Bros and other 526 proprietors, asking them to confer with the object of deciding between themselves how the reduction should be apportioned.

On 10 March the West London Association (Route 526) proprietors held a meeting and unanimously resolved to take no action whatever.

On 18 March, in reply to a letter from the Minister, Birch Bros wrote opposing the proposed reduction of Route 526 to

a half-hourly service and observing that the proposal completely ignored the wishes of the local inhabitants who were
strongly opposed to any reduction of service. It also ignored
the through facilities which had been previously unavailable
to the public, who previously had to change at Horn Lane,
Acton, and at Cricklewood Broadway. The gravamen of Birch
Bros' complaint was, however, that the reduction constituted
a gross breach of faith in view of:

(1) The Minister's statement in the House on 12 March
1925, undertaking to avoid injustices.

(2) Mr Bassom's statement on 7 April 1925, when he
handed my father a list of routes upon which he
could operate omnibuses provided he commenced his
services quickly, and

(3) Sir Henry Jackson's statement on behalf of the Minister
in the House on 21 May 1925, that: 'All proprietors
injured by the first restrictions had been found new
routes and were satisfied.'

On 30 March the Minister wrote to Birch Bros announcing
that their journeys on Route 526 would be reduced from
fifteen per day, ie a reduction of three omnibuses to one. At
the same time the Minister refused to receive a deputation
from the WLA Route 526 proprietors.

To sum up, the Minister's idea appeared to be roughly that
one independent omnibus should be withdrawn to every two
LGOC buses. This worked out that independents, who provided eleven per cent of all omnibuses in London, should be
reduced by $33\frac{1}{3}$ per cent, while Route 526, all independent
proprietors, should be reduced by $66\frac{2}{3}$ per cent. It was clear
from this that the main issue was not protection of trams but
the crushing of independents.

On 1 April the matter was debated in the House of Commons,
during which the Minister, in reply to Captain Ian Fraser, MP
for North St Pancras, stated that 'the Honourable Members
will find that in the end very little injustice will really be
done.'

It will be remembered that May 1926 was the month and

year of the General Strike. With regard to this, it is a fact that whilst nearly the whole of the LGOC's fleet of omnibuses were left in their garages, nearly all the omnibuses of the Independent Omnibus Proprietors were at work with volunteer drivers and conductors. Birch Bros can claim that during that crisis they worked 100 per cent of their fleet.

In September 1926 proceedings were taken against Cornelius Beatty in the Ealing Police Court because he refused to comply with the Minister's order and remove his omnibus from Route 17, for which the Police held his schedule. This case was dismissed and costs given against the Police. An appeal was made by the Police Authorities to the High Court, when the Justices were directed to convict.

No proceedings were ever instituted against the proprietors of omnibuses on Route 526, and subsequently the Order was cancelled.

In 1927 a company with the title London Public Omnibus Co Ltd was formed, and about half of the independent omnibus operators, discouraged by the manner in which they felt they were treated by the Ministry of Transport, sold their vehicles and their goodwill to that company.

Very soon afterwards, it was found that the control of the London Public Omnibus Co Ltd had become vested in the LGOC.

In November 1926, Birch Bros were approached by Mr Robert Thackray to join him in opening a new route of omnibuses, between Pimlico (Bessborough Gardens) and Hampstead Heath via Belsize Park, Ladbroke Grove and Shepherds Bush, for the approval of which he had made application to the Commissioner of Police on 4 November, but which was refused by the Commissioner a fortnight later on the grounds that it traversed certain restricted streets.

On 30 November 1926, application was made by Birch Bros to the Commissioner of Police for the same route (eliminating from the route the restricted street 'Southend Green' at the Hampstead end of it), and on 8 December Birch Bros wrote to the Commissioner of Police pointing out the lack of bus connection between Haverstock Hill and Swiss Cottage (over a mile), and the absence of direct facilities between Swiss Cottage and Ladbroke Grove, or between Harrow Road and Shepherds Bush; and directing his attention to the fact that the portions of restricted streets which the route traversed were negligible, being a matter of only 160 yds of High Road, Kilburn, and twenty yds of Harrow Road (as between Kilburn Lane and Ladbroke Grove).

It was pointed out that the populous neighbourhood of Harrow Road was entirely unserved in the directions indicated; moreover, that Birch Bros proposed to place upon the route pneumatic-tyred new single-deck omnibuses.

This application was refused, and in reply to Birch Bros' request in January 1927 for reasons of such refusal, they were informed that the traversing and crossing of busy congested restricted thoroughfares as would be occasioned by the operation of this route would be against the convenience of traffic.

Birch Bros then realised that if they were to succeed in applications for new routes it would be necessary for them to have the required buses in existence and licensed, so that if and when a route were granted they could commence operations immediately, otherwise there was a grave danger that during the delay in obtaining chassis and getting bodies built a Street Restriction Order might be brought in, restricting streets on the proposed route. Accordingly, on 29 January 1927, Birch Bros placed an order with Dennis Bros for six single-deck chassis.

A letter dated 18 February 1927, was sent from the Paddington Borough Council directed to the Association of London Omnibus Proprietors, drawing attention to the lack of omnibus facilities between Maida Vale and Queen's Road, Bayswater, since the withdrawal of LGOC's service No 74, and urging the need of the reinstatement of such facilities.

The letter was passed to Birch Bros by the Secretary of the Association of London Omnibus Proprietors and my father saw the town clerk on 4 March 1927, following up his call by

a letter on 9 March, offering to provide a service between
Hampstead Heath and Hammersmith, Brook Green, following
old Route 74 as between Maida Vale and Queen's Road to
Brook Green (Maida Vale to Queen's Road only being too
short a route to be worked economically).

On 9 April Birch Bros wrote to the secretary of the
Ministry of Transport, informing him that they had received
representations from the public, Paddington Borough Council,
Paddington and Bayswater Chamber of Commerce, Messrs
Whiteley Ltd, etc, asking for an omnibus service between
Maida Vale and Queen's Road in particular, and that Birch
Bros had discussed with them a proposed route from Hampstead to Brook Green and alternatively to Red Lion, Barnes;
expressing willingness to provide an adequate service of
single-deck, low-loading, pneumatic-tyred omnibuses on the
route and urging, in view of the strong recommendation
and complete absence of direct communication between
Hampstead and Maida Vale, that such service would be of
public value and would not cause congestion. It was pointed
out that the proposed route traversed very few restricted
streets and it was suggested that the necessary amendment
of restriction order be made.

A reply was received from the Ministry of Transport, dated
12 May, stating that no decision had been reached, and on
28 July my father and my brother interviewed Inspector
May, of the Public Carriage Office, Metropolitan Police, and
understood that if the Ministry of Transport made the necessary restricted streets amendment order, the Police would
probably waive any objection to the route on the score of
inconvenience to traffic.

On 15 August my father and my brother interviewed Mr
E.M. Phillips, of the Ministry of Transport, when they were
given to understand that the London and Home Counties
Traffic Advisory Committee objected on principle to any
additional omnibuses in London.

On 19 August a letter was received from the Ministry of
Transport, intimating that no decision had yet been reached

but that the Minister would not view with favour any proposal involving additional omnibuses being placed into service in the Paddington area.

In 1927, while negotiations in this matter were still proceeding, Birch Bros Ltd was approached by a company developing an estate in the Greenford area to provide a service from there to Ealing Broadway; the route proposed was not approved by the Commissioner of Police because of alleged excessive road camber and roadside obstructions, but, in the same week as it was refused, Route 141, Edgware and Boreham Wood, was approved by the Commissioner of Police to the LGOC although the camber, obstructions and other disabilities were far more serious than in the case of the Ealing route proposed by Birch Bros Ltd.

This matter, together with the matter of the route from Hampstead and Maida Vale, was brought to the notice of the Assistant Commissioner by William Henry Birch at an interview, and eventually a modified route between Belsize Park (Hampstead), Maida Vale, and Kensal Rise, was approved by the Commissioner of Police in December 1927, as Route 203 (later to develop into Route 231).

Birch Bros Ltd, however, did not abandon its intention to continue to press for the diversion of this route to serve Westbourne Grove and Shepherds Bush.

Schedules were deposited and operation on Route 203 was commenced at the end of December 1927.

During the first quarter of 1928 several other proprietors scheduled one or two omnibuses each for operation on Route 203, and in addition, the London Public Omnibus Co Ltd (which had been formed the previous year with the backing of Mr Hatry and the Marquis of Winchester, with the object of purchasing as many independent omnibuses as possible, and had unsuccessfully approached Birch Bros for the purchase of its omnibuses), scheduled first four then eight omnibuses for operation on this route. It must have been obvious to the London Public Omnibus Co Ltd that a route that was likely to be remunerative for a proprietor operating a ten-minute service (which Birch Bros Ltd was doing) could not possibly be remunerative if the total frequency of service averaged three minutes, so that their action was regarded by Birch Bros as intended to be merely damaging, which was borne out by the chasing tactics adopted by them. In spite of this heavy competition, and the additional omnibuses which Birch Bros Ltd had to place in service to deal with it, the revenue per car mile remained fairly stationary after the first quarter.

In March 1928, a number of roads traversed by the route were scheduled as Restricted Streets by the Ministry of Transport. Shortly afterwards Birch Bros asked the Commissioner of Police for his approval of the extension of the route from Belsize Park to Hampstead Heath, which was the terminal originally proposed by Birch Bros for the proposed route between Hampstead, Maida Vale, Westbourne Grove and Shepherds Bush, and in May 1928, the extended route was approved by the Commissioner as Route 231, and Birch Bros commenced to operate it as a Sunday service only (Sunday being a day upon which Restricted Streets Regulations did not apply), and it being impossible to operate the extended service on weekdays without the dispensation of the Minister, on account of the extended portion traversing Haverstock Hill, which had been scheduled by the Minister of Transport as a Restricted Street before the commencement of operations on Route 203. Immediately afterwards Birch Bros applied to the Minister for a dispensation to operate the extended route daily with, however, a diversion of route via Englands Lane and Haverstock Hill to avoid the residential Belsize Park Gardens, and to provide a service to and from Belsize Park Underground Station. This application was refused, but the negotiations followed, and almost immediately a further application was made to the Minister for a dispensation to operate a modified route between Hampstead Town Hall and Kensal Rise. This also was refused, but following negotiations, a modified route between Hampstead Town Hall and Kensal Rise (involving one-way operation at the Hampstead end anti-clockwise, via Englands Lane, Haverstock Hill, and Belsize Park Gardens), was approved in December 1928 by the Commissioner of Police as Route 231A, a dispensation was granted by the Minister of Transport; and a weekly service commenced.

At the end of December 1928, Birch Bros applied to the Commissioner of Police and the Minister of Transport for their approval and dispensation respectively, in regard to a proposed daily extension of the service from Kensal Rise to Harlesden.

In the first quarter of 1929, Birch Bros' receipts per car mile commenced to increase, (a) partly because the LGOC having completely absorbed the London Public Omnibus Co Ltd's operations, withdrew their service (presumably because of the heavy losses it had sustained), (b) partly because as a consequence Birch Bros was able temporarily to reduce its own service (which had been increased to deal with the London Public Omnibus Co's competition), with a consequent saving in running costs, and (c) partly because the service had been extended one stage nearer its natural and proper terminal at Hampstead Heath.

In February 1929, Birch Bros' proposal for extension to Harlesden was rejected by the Commissioner of Police. In June 1929, and again in September 1929, they made application to the Minister for dispensation to operate the full route, Hampstead Heath and Kensal Rise, on weekdays as well as Sundays, but without success.

At the end of 1929 the Minister granted a dispensation to the LGOC to operate additional omnibuses between Kensal Rise and Willesden, upon a route competitive with Route 231, thereby damaging Birch Bros' traffic from Kensal Rise.

In January 1930, in view of the damaging effect of the additional service permitted the LGOC between Kensal Rise and Willesden, Birch Bros applied to the Minister of Transport and the Commissioner of Police for their dispensation and approval respectively for an extension of Route 231 daily to Willesden; the extension Hampstead Town Hall and Willesden was approved by the Commissioner in February as

Route 231, and a service commenced on Sundays only.

At the end of February, as a consequence of Birch Bros' application for dispensation (upon which the Minister had given no decision), and as a result of the difficulties on Route 214 which I will mention later, they were introduced by the Minister of Transport to the LGOC with a view of settlement.

In July 1930, Birch Bros reported to the Minister that negotiations had broken down largely on the question of the extension from Kensal Rise to Willesden, but immediately afterwards they made a further proposal to the Minister for his reconsideration of the extension to Harlesden, which was proposed in 1928, and negotiations were resumed.

In December 1930, as a result of extended negotiations with the Commissioner, the Minister and the LGOC and with the support of the Hampstead Borough Council (who were anxious to avoid the annoyance caused to residents by buses traversing Downshire Hill and Belsize Park Gardens, the two roads concerned in the one-way operation at the Hampstead end, which Birch Bros itself had always desired to eliminate), Birch Bros obtained the approval of the Commissioner and the Minister's dispensation for operation of extended Route 231, Hampstead Heath (South End Green) and Harlesden, as a daily service.

This result was part of the Co-ordination Agreement arrived at between Birch Bros and the LGOC which I will mention later.

Birch Bros made application for permission to operate double-deck omnibuses upon this route instead of single-deck omnibuses. This application was originally made in June 1931, when the Commissioner of Police replied that he would be able to accede to the application provided certain roadside obstructions were removed, or suitably modified. A number of alterations having been made by the local authorities during the course of road-making and repair on portions of the road, Birch Bros made a further application in June 1933, pointing out the improved conditions. Since that application the authority in such matters had been transferred to the Metropolitan Traffic Commissioner, who replied that when the obstructions referred to in the Commissioner's letter of 1931 were dealt with, he would be prepared to give his approval.

Birch Bros then submitted to the Metropolitan Traffic Commissioner a drawing of a modified double-deck vehicle, of which the upper deck was considerably inset on the near side so as to avoid all possible obstructions with as great ease as with single-deck omnibuses. They had also prepared a superstructure for attachment to a single-deck omnibus with which to demonstrate the effectiveness of the proposed arrangement, but awaited in vain an appointment to test the route with this equipment.

Had Birch Bros been permitted to operate double-deck omnibuses on this route, it was their intention to provide vehicles with oil engines.

Coincidentally with the development of the above services was that of Route 214 in the Hendon-Mill Hill area.

From the moment that construction was commenced on the relevant portions of the Watford and Barnet by-pass road, Birch Bros had formulated a plan for an entirely new omnibus route between Hendon Central, Mill Hill and Edgware, and on 18 October 1928, the day that the Hendon and Mill Hill section of the by-pass road was open for traffic, Birch Bros made application to the Commissioner of Police for the approval of a route which was eventually approved by the Commissioner as Route 214, Hendon Central and Canons Park, for operation by single-deck omnibuses, the roads covered not being Restricted Streets under the London Traffic Act 1924.

At the end of October 1928, schedules were deposited and operation was commenced, the full route being covered by a few journeys only. The bulk of the journeys were operated on the section of the route between Hendon Central and Edgware. The whole of the route was through developed or partially developed neighbourhoods, a very high proportion of it following the new Watford by-pass road.

Immediately after the commencement, a number of roads traversed were scheduled as Restricted Streets by the Minister of Transport.

In the second quarter of 1929 the short journeys were extended, and the whole service was operated between Hendon Central and Canons Park.

On 1 February 1929, Birch Bros had indicated to the Commissioner of Police their willingness to increase the frequency of the service in view of a suggestion by a member of the public that the service on the Hendon-Mill Hill section was inadequate, and shortly afterwards, they applied to the Minister of Transport for a dispensation to operate additional journeys; this application was supported by reference to additional journeys permitted to the LGOC on the Mill Hill-Edgware section of Route 104, which was a route competitive to a small extent with Route 214. In April, Birch Bros heard that the LGOC had applied to the Minister for dispensation to operate an entirely new service from the West End to Mill Hill via the Hendon-Mill Hill section of Route 214, and immediately objected to this proposed service as being unnecessary between Hendon and Mill Hill, since Route 214, possibly with some slight increase, was quite capable of dealing with the traffic.

Considerable correspondence with the Minister followed, during the course of which Birch Bros requested the Minister to cause a census to be taken of the loadings on Route 214, in order to satisfy himself that the new LGOC service was unnecessary, to which request he did not accede. Birch Bros also offered on more than one occasion to work a co-ordinated service with the LGOC between Mill Hill, Hendon Central and the West End, should the Minister consider that a through omnibus service between Mill Hill and the West End was necessary, and expressed willingness to provide such a service, as they understood that this was the condition by which the LGOC were from time to time permitted to operate new services. Birch Bros asked the Minister to exercise his discretion judicially and fairly between themselves and the LGOC and asked to be accorded an opportunity of attending before the London & Home Counties Traffic Advisory Committee (which was the body responsible for advising the Minister on such matters). This request was granted and my father was invited to attend the Advisory Committee to state Birch Bros' case in regard to their Routes 214 and 231. As a consequence of that interview Birch Bros put forward an alternative scheme for an extended Route 214 between Mill Hill and Victoria, proposing to withdraw the omnibuses for such extension from other routes, but on 1 August this proposal was rejected, and Birch Bros thereupon wrote to the Minister asking in what way their proposal failed to meet his reasonable requirements, and what modified proposal would be acceptable to him, expressing their willingness to collaborate with the Minister and Commissioner of Police with a view to disposing of the matter, but obtained no satisfactory reply.

As a result of Birch Bros' own difficulties and those of other independent proprietors, the new Minister (Herbert Morrison) received a deputation on 30 September 1929, following which, at his request, copies of the whole correspondence were sent to him.

In the meanwhile, towards the end of the June quarter 1929, the LGOC with the Minister's permission, commenced operating a new route No 121, between Mill Hill, Hendon Central, Oxford Circus and Dulwich, equal in frequency to the service operated by Birch Bros as between Hendon and Mill Hill, and in the September quarter this competition naturally affected the development of Birch Bros' service adversely. At the same time, although restrictions had been raised in favour of LGOC to permit this competition, Birch Bros were prevented by the Restricted Streets Regulations of the London Traffic Act from adopting the normal competitive course of immediately extending their Route 214 over the LGOC route into the West End.

In the March quarter of 1930 the LGOC split their Route 121 at Hendon Central in order to run a short service directly in opposition to Birch Bros between Hendon Central and Mill Hill, and while the remainder of the service from Hendon Central to the West End continued to be operated by old type double-deck vehicles, the latest and fastest type of six-cylinder single-deck vehicles were allocated by the LGOC to their short Route 121E, Hendon Central and Mill Hill, with the object of chasing and damaging the service of Birch Bros as much as possible. The splitting of Route 121 at Hendon Central also had the effect of doubling the number of services terminating on the authorised stand there, and this added to the difficulties of Birch Bros, as their vehicles were always pushed off the stand by the LGOC omnibuses to prevent them having an opportunity to wait for passengers outside the Station. Also an LGOC inspector was permanently stationed at Mill Hill in order to ensure that an LGOC omnibus always left the stand just before one of Birch Bros' omnibuses as it arrived from Edgware. Faced with this heavy competition (and being prevented by the London Traffic Act from dealing with it adequately), Birch Bros decided in the June quarter of 1930 temporarily to shorten the bulk of the journeys so as to terminate at Edgware instead of Canons Park, thus effecting a saving in running costs and increasing the receipts per car mile.

Throughout this competition Birch Bros experienced very gratifying loyalty from the local public, who undoubtedly favoured the Birch Bros Route 214 against the LGOC Route 121E.

As a consequence of Birch Bros continuing pressure upon the LGOC they were in February 1930 asked by the Minister to meet the directors with a view to an amicable settlement of this and other matters, as the Minister's action in permitting the inauguration on Route 121 by the LGOC had resulted in a most unsatisfactory condition of affairs. In March 1930, Birch Bros wrote to the Minister, as they had had no reply to their letter to him of the previous 30 September, and at the same time informed him of the damaging revision of Route 121. Further correspondence followed, during which, following a breakdown of the negotiations with the LGOC, Birch Bros almost succeeded in getting the Minister's approval of a modified route to the West End, terminating at Portman Square or Baker Street. The Minister, however, changed his mind at the last moment and negotiations with the LGOC were resumed.

As I have already mentioned, an agreement was eventually arrived at (August 1930) between Birch Bros and the LGOC, by which the whole of Birch Bros' routes were co-ordinated with those of the LGOC. By virtue of that agreement, Birch Bros on 31 December 1930, abandoned the section of Route 214 between Mill Hill and Edgware, while the LGOC, withdrew their omnibuses from Route 121E, Mill Hill and Hendon Central, and Birch Bros became solely responsible for the omnibus service between Mill Hill and Hendon Central via the by-pass road, and considerably increased the frequency of service on Route 214C (which became the number of the shortened route), at the same time agreeing to replace single-deck omnibuses by double-deck omnibuses as soon as the latter could be obtained, which was speedily done.

The LGOC during their operation of Route 121E had instituted a system of through booking tickets (including season tickets), which were available for transfer at the combined fare between their omnibuses and the Underground system, and it was a condition of the agreement that Birch Bros took over the provision of these facilities. As a consequence of agreement being reached, the intensity of the LGOC competition was relaxed in the December of 1930, inasmuch as while Route 121E continued to operate until the date of co-ordination, yet such operation was conducted in as amicable a manner as possible.

As a result of the economies effected in the first half of the year, of the relaxation of competition towards the end of the year, and of the rapid development of the whole neighbourhood served, the receipts showed considerable improvement.

The receipts per car mile during the years 1931 and 1932 continued to show a steady upward movement, although the service had been somewhat increased from time to time.

Late in the June quarter of 1933 it was deemed desirable to increase the service during slack hours in order to provide a more even headway (a minimum of ten-minute intervals except late in the evening).

The immediate effect of this in the September of 1933 added to the usual seasonal phenomenon of a slight drop in traffic during the holiday quarter of the year (particularly noticeable in a purely residential surburban district as that served), was that the increase in mileage caused a temporary decrease in receipts per car mile, as expected, but it was anticipated that the additional mileage, in a short time, would itself have fructified, and resulted in a still further increase of traffic.

The agreement which was reached with the LGOC on 7 August 1930, provided that Birch Bros' operations on Routes 284A, 227, 26D and 266 should be surrendered to the LGOC, and that the LGOC on their part withdrew their services on Route 121E (Route 214) and found room for two more double-deck omnibuses on Route 526D by withdrawing two of theirs. In the last paragraph of his letter of that date, Mr Pick wrote, 'Perhaps you will state whether you think we need a formal agreement to give effect to our understanding', and in his reply on 11 August my father wrote, 'I think the arrangements could quite well rest upon letters between us and that a formal agreement should be unnecessary.'

Arrangements were made consequent upon the agreement for through bookings between Birch Bros' service on Route 214 and the Underground Railways.

The full agreement came into operation on 31 December 1930.

It should be borne in mind that these working arrangements with the LGOC came about as a result of the difficulties which arose from the operation of the London Traffic Act. Although that Act had been designed to suppress over-competition, it resulted, to some extent at any rate, in a form of intensified competition within the limits of the provisions of the Act. Moreover, there was a certain amount of discrimination in the working of the Act. In consequence, it came about that an increasing competition arose between the LGOC and Birch Bros, particularly on Route 214; the LGOC obtained sanction to run a short route directly along the course of Route 214, and by 'sandwiching' Birch Bros' buses between theirs, and 'crowding' at stopping places, they were successful in their opposition and the receipts from Birch Bros' buses were seriously affected. As a result, Birch Bros had to reduce their mileage on this route to make it payable. The culmination of this competition on Route 214 — together with a certain amount of contention over other routes — was for negotiations to take place between them and the LGOC, which eventually led to the Co-ordination Agreement of August 1930.

By the time I joined the Company in 1932 the hectic days on the road were past and the fight was transferred to Parliament. With the passing of the London Passenger Transport Act 1933, this fight was lost and our London operations ceased on 10 February 1934, with the compulsory purchase of our twentyeight buses.

We started with open-top, solid-tyred, normal-control 48-seater buses looking very much like their 1906 counterparts, and finished only nine years later with covered-top, pneumatic-tyred, forward-control 56-seater diesel-engined double-deck buses, looking very much like their counterparts today. In no other decade, before or since, has bus design improved so fast as during the 'Roaring Twenties', and for this improvement the London independents were largely responsible.

EDINBURGH EXPERIMENTAL VEHICLES

Gavin A. Booth

Mr Booth, an active member of the Omnibus Society, is today Honorary Editor of the Society's publications, including the monthly Omnibus Magazine. *In this paper, which was read to the Scottish Branch of the Society in 1963, he surveys the contribution that Edinburgh has made to the technical development of passenger transport, and in particular the work of the Corporation's transport undertaking. Mr Booth is Book Production Assistant with Ian Allan, the transport publishers.*

Edinburgh transport department over the years has, in common with most other comparable municipalities, carried out numerous experiments of varying importance, many of which have had a decided influence on later deliveries. As will be seen, two specific periods, the early 30s and the post-1950 era, are particularly abundant in such experiments, but perhaps it would be relevant to start with a brief resumé of early passenger transport in Edinburgh.

Forgetting stage-coaches and cabs, the first recorded attempt to transport the citizens of Victorian Edinburgh in any quantity was made by R.W. Thomson, who carried out trials of a steam-bus of 'elegant construction and appearance' in the Granton area in 1869. It was a 65-seater, and the contemporary press noted 'the dexterity with which it picked its way between cart horses, omnibuses and cabs, and the docility with which it stopped or turned whenever it was required.' The Thomson Road Steamer was placed in service on the Portobello route, preceded by a man on horseback with a red flag. A rival machine was produced by A. Nairn of

Bowershall Engine Works. The ill-fated inventor managed to persuade the Provost of Leith to come for a run and the Provost brought along the Leith magistrates and councillors for company. They decided on a day at the seaside, and proceeded to Cramond. The outward journey was uneventful, and after a lunch on council expenses at the Cramond Brig Hotel, they set back for town, but an axle broke near the Dean Park toll-bar, and the bus was towed back to Leith — by horse.

The Edinburgh Tramways Act of 1871 authorised the laying of rails 'and the use of animal power only' (as far as researches show, only horses took advantage of this). Edinburgh Corporation leased the rails to the newly-formed Edinburgh Street Tramway Company, and the first service of horse cars started on 6 November 1871 between Bernard Street and Haymarket. An experiment of ten years later involved the use of a steam tram, specially permitted by the town council, on the Post Office-Portobello route. Only one vehicle — rather like an early railway locomotive — was ever operated, coupled to passenger-carrying trailers. In September 1882 permission was sought to convert the whole Portobello route to steam, but the residents of Portobello had had enough, and permission was refused.

On 28 January 1888 the Edinburgh Northern Cable Tramways Company inaugurated the city's first cablecar service, between Hanover Street and Goldenacre, the incline being too much even for Edinburgh horses. Eight Metropolitan-Cammell cars were used for this route, and eight smaller cars from Falcon followed in 1890 for their other route from Frederick Street to Comely Bank. To confuse things even more, Edinburgh Corporation purchased all the Edinburgh Street Tramways lines within their area, and leased them to Dick Kerr & Company in 1893, who operated over them on a joint basis with the Edinburgh & District Tramways Company. Then in 1897 the Corporation purchased the Northern company, and leased their lines to the Edinburgh District company.

Before we get too entangled, let us examine the place of the motor-bus at this time. In 1898 a licence was granted to John Love to operate 8-seat Daimlers between the GPO and Haymarket. He gave up in 1901, and the Edinburgh Autocar Company took over. They gave up in 1902, and Rossleigh took over; they in turn gave up after a few months. The day of the bus, it seemed, had yet to come in Edinburgh. The next recorded operation of motor-buses was in 1904, when Stirlings Motor Cars took over a factory at Granton and built a machine called the Kingsburgh. Some of these vehicles were placed in service between the GPO and Haymarket, but perhaps merely as an advertisement, since this company is reputed to have built psvs for use in London. The Kingsburgh was a 12-seater, and the driving position was above the engine.

Meanwhile, since nearby Leith Corporation and the Musselburgh & District Electric Light & Traction Company were following the national trend and operating electric tramcars, Edinburgh Corporation decided to convert its entire system — to cable operation. In 1896 the company constructed a completely new type of vehicle, with two lever brakes and a gripper stand with a spoked driving wheel. This car, number 112 was the prototype of the majority of Edinburgh's later cable cars. At its height, the Edinburgh cable system was one of the largest in the world, as well as a standard joke over most of Scotland. (Stories are told of the gentleman who, tired of being marooned in a cable car on the North Bridge, stormed off, taking the immense gripper wheel, and of the old woman who underestimated the speed of the car and tumbled off in a heap. 'Och, it disnae maitter,' she murmured, 'a' wis gettin' off onywey!' A transport department veteran summed it all up by suggesting that 'the fellows who invented the cable system should have been presented with gold medals — and then lined up and shot!') On 1 June 1899 the Lord Provost and members of the tramways committee boarded new cable car 142 at Shrubhill, and at the sound of the one o'clock gun they moved off with typical

Edinburgh ceremony for St Andrew Square. For the rest of that day free rides were given to the curious public, partly for publicity reasons but mainly because the Board of Trade certificate had not yet arrived. Edinburgh & District were not, however, blind to the advantages of electric traction, since they started running four bogie electric cars between Ardmillan Terrace and Slatedord in 1910, not as an experiment, but because the Tollcross power station could not generate sufficient power to operate a cable at that distance. The cars had to be towed to and from Shrubhill by cable car.

In 1914 Edinburgh Corporation purchased their first buses — three Leylands and three Tilling Stevens for a Blackford Hill-Marchmont-Meadows-Dalkeith Road-Mayfield circular route. These were short-lived, since in 1916 the War Department requisitioned the Leylands, and the Tilling Stevens passed to Scottish Motor Traction and later to the Birmingham & Midland Motor Omnibus Company.

DEVELOPMENT BETWEEN THE WARS

The Edinburgh & District Tramways Company's lease expired in 1919, and when Edinburgh Corporation took over it was decided to convert the cable system to electricity, and at the same time the newly-appointed transport manager, R. Stuart Pilcher, decided to purchase some charabancs for touring and some 31-seat buses to supplement cable cars in the event of the frequent breakdowns. He also inaugurated the corporation's first regular bus service between Abbeyhill and Ardmillan Terrace. All but one of the vehicles supplied in 1919-20 were Leylands, the 'intruder' being an AEC Y with Hora body, whose successful operation led to the purchase of twentynine similar vehicles in 1921. Spurred on by the success of the motor-bus, Edinburgh Corporation followed up in 1922 by purchasing an AEC 403 double-decker with Brush 54-seat open-top body, 193 (NO5027). This vehicle had originally been an AEC demonstrator, and was soon joined by 192 (SG4869), a similar vehicle, which had started with the corporation as a Fry-bodied single-decker but which was short-lived in this guise.

The same year, 1922, witnessed two important landmarks in the Edinburgh tramway story. In June of that year the first 'modern' electric service, from Stanley Road to Nether Liberton, was started, and October saw the remarkable over-night conversion of Princes Street from cable to electric operation. The former event was marked by the usual Edin-burgh ceremony mentioned above, this time in the form of a soot and flour raid by students on the car containing the Lord Provost and town council, and a police baton charge. Almost exactly one year after this, the very last cable car trundled from the Post Office to Portobello 'almost unnoticed.' The completion of the cable-electric conversion enabled the corporation to evolve a standard tramcar best suited to their needs. Apart from a number of converted cable cars, the standard car was built by the corporation and outside makers between 1922 and 1931. Various experiments with these cars over the years contributed towards the improvement of the breed. Normally, they were on Peckham P22 trucks with Metropolitan Vickers 101 motors, and originally were open-balconied. Several different motors were tried, but because of the tendency for motors to become mixed through over-hauls, etc, it is difficult to trace these on individual cars. It is known, however, that 132 ran with a General Electric 265 motor around 1923, and 205 was fitted with a British Thomson Houston 509 in 1928. In 1926 a start was made fitting transverse upholstered seats in these cars instead of the usual longitudinal wooden ones, since the public had shown a 'decided preference' for them.

The next development came in 1929 when the transport committee approved the enclosing of the open-balcony on one car, 70, which was inspected later that year and approved. Corporation-built 367 of the same year was the first new totally-enclosed car to present itself to the scrutiny of the Edinburgh public; the transport committee minutes reported: 'the totally-enclosed or All-weather cars are adding materially to the comfort of the travelling public, particularly during inclement weather.' Other experiments involved the fitting of regenerative equipment to certain cars on the Musselburgh route in 1932, of bow-collectors to 67, 110 and 170 in 1925-6, and a pantograph to 73 in 1933. 73 plus pantograph successfully brought down the wiring outside Portobello depot.

Meanwhile, little was happening on the bus front. In 1925 all-night buses were introduced for one experimental week. Night buses are still with us over forty years later, so the experiment must have been successful. The years 1923-5 yielded no new buses, but 1926 produced Dennis charabancs, the first of a number of Leyland PLSC Lions, and the experimental AEC double-deckers of 1922 bore fruit in the shape of four AEC 507s with Brush bodies, notable in having pneumatic front and solid rear tyres. Standard vehicles over the next few years were the Leyland Lions, 6-wheel Karrier WL6s and the basically similar ADC 423 and AEC Reliance models with variety provided by a batch of Dennis coaches. The shape of things to come was forecast in 1929 when a Croall-bodied Daimler CF6 (SC3416) was purchased, proving successful in so far as thirtyfive of these chassis were purchased in 1930 and thirteen more in 1931. Still not satisfied that the Daimler CF6 was the ultimate for their needs, Edinburgh Corporation continued to experiment. SC8791 of 1930 was a Daimler CH6 double-deck chassis with preselective gearbox – Edinburgh's first – and Hume single-deck body, while 1931 heralded three experimental vehicles with similar bodies by Alexander of Edinburgh. These were a Crossley Alpha, an Albion PMB28 and a Daimler CP6 (SC9901-3). 1932's orders contained a number of Morris Commercials, including two Metropolitan-Cammell metal-framed Dictators. Further Morris Commercials followed in 1933 – two Dictators with Metro-Cammell and English Electric bodies, and one Imperial double-decker with Park Royal 50-seat body (FS6340), Edinburgh's first 'modern' double-decker and one of the city's only two lowbridge vehicles, the other being a similar chassis with a steel Metro-Cammell body of 1934 (FS9611).

In the early 30s, many operators were awakening to the advantages of the diesel engine but in 1931 three Leyland Lions were converted to tar-oil operation. They were used for several months on the 12 route (Surgeons Hall-Portobello), but since they required 'de-gumming' every month, they were not the success expected. Edinburgh did, however, come round to experimenting in 1933 with a six-cylinder Beardmore oil unit in SC3430, a 1929 AEC Reliance. The next year the remainder of the Reliances received four-cylinder AEC oil engines, while SC7301, a 1930 Daimler CF6, got a Thornycroft, and the 1931 Crossley and Albion received Crossley and Gardner units respectively. The 1934 orders featured new diesel vehicles, all experimental. FS7036, originally exhibited at the 1933 Commercial Show, was a Daimler COG5 with Weymann body; WS637 a Daimler COT4 with four-cylinder Tangye engine and Roberts body; and WS1508 an AEC Q with Weymann body.

After several years of apparent indecision, the transport department decided that the Gardner 5LW was the perfect single-deck unit, and the 6LW its double-deck counterpart. 1935-9 produced sixtythree Daimler COG5s with Weymann bodies, and fiftyone Metro-Cammell bodied COG6s.

The bus fleet settled down for the time being so we now jump back to 1932, and find the tram fleet in a sad state of uncertainty. The last completely new wooden standards appeared in 1932, 250-9, Pickering-built cars with Maley & Taunton Sing-Link trucks except 256, which was fitted experimentally with an English Electric truck. The same year saw one of the more important experiments in Edinburgh's tramway story. This was the appearance of 'Red Biddy,' the Shrubhill-built steel car, 180. 180, painted bright red and grey, was an attractively austere 64-seater, originally on an EMB truck but later transferred to a Maley & Taunton Swing-Link. However much the colour scheme may have shocked the staid residents of Joppa and Corstorphine on the 12 route where it originally saw service, 'Red Biddy' was eminently successful and attracted much comment. It was described as 'the nearest thing to perpetual motion' by an observer, and as 'very satisfactory' by the corporation. Outside builders were then commissioned to build further steel cars, and 1932 saw 260/5 from MCW, of similar design to 180. MCW also produced 241/2/4-6/9 with domed roofs, and Hurst Nelson 231/9/40 in the same style. All the outside-built cars were on Swing-Link trucks, some with MV101 motors and others with Dick Kerr 84 units. A notable feature of the Metro-Cammell domed-roof cars was the fitment of swivel seats. Experimental operation of these cars led to the development of a new standard steel car, but while the Shrubhill designers went ahead, further orders were placed with outside firms for twentythree new steel cars. When these materialised, they were all of similar design, an attractive streamlined type on Swing-Link, P22 and English Electric trucks. They were built by Hurst Nelson (11-8), English Electric (19-24, 262/3/7) and Metro-Cammell (25-30). For variety, trucks and motors were well-mixed, but basically with a liberal distribution of Metro-Vick 101 and Dick Kerr 84 motors, the MCW cars and English Electric 262/3 had Swing-Link trucks and the remainder, save for 267, had Peckham P22s. 267 originally had the English Electric truck from 256, but later received a standard P22, while 21-4 soon received Swing-Links to replace their P22s. The majority of these cars, in common with other steel experimental cars, entered service on service 7 (Liberton-Stanley Road), which was regarded as a 'guinea pig' route in much the way as the 19 Circle was used for bus experiments in the 1950s. December 1934 saw the appearance of 69, the first of eightyfour similar Shrubhill-built steel standards which were produced in varying quantities over the years to 1950, and incorporated the best features proved in their various steel predecessors. In appearance they could be described as a cross between the 1932 domed-roof cars and the 1934 streamliners, and were among the most elegant cars built for service in Britain in the 1930s.

The outbreak of war in 1939 meant the discontinuance of the standard Daimler/MCW combination in the bus fleet and a slowing-down of tramcar production, although between 1940-5 eight new cars were scraped together. Even in the first years of the war, before the normal 'utility' vehicles were available, Edinburgh had obtained two AEC Regent/ Park Royal double-deckers, two Tilling Stevens/Willowbrook saloons, one Bristol L5G/Bristol saloon, and one Leyland TD7/Pickering and one Bristol K5G/Northern Counties, in a fleet where none of these makes was standard. Obviously with a war in progress, and the bus fleet being augmented by three types of utility vehicles with seven makes of body, little could be done in the experimental line. The fitting of nine Daimler COG5 saloons with gas trailers was merely to satisfy the percentage of such conversions required by the Ministry of War Transport.

THE POST-WAR YEARS

With the return of peace, the first thought was towards the restoration of the bus fleet to its pre-war level. The most readily available buses were purchased and standardisation was meantime sacrificed. The bulk of vehicles purchased between 1947 and 1951 were Birmingham-style Daimler CVG6s, although there were also CVD6s, CVG5 single-deckers, Guy Arab saloons and double-deckers, with AEC Regents, Bedford OBs and Crossley SD42s thrown in for good measure. The only experiment recorded on any of these vehicles was the fitting of unpainted glassfibre domes on 236, one of the Regents, when it received a new upper deck after an argument with a low bridge. With an eye to the future, however, several demonstrators were operated for varying periods. First post-war example was a Daimler/Willowbrook 35-seater, FRW587, of 1947, followed the next year by FHP540, a similar vehicle. Other demonstrators tried during this period were ACN794, an all-Guy saloon and GHP259, another CVD6, this time a Northern Coachbuilders-bodied double-decker.

This, meanwhile, was the time of the acceptance of the underfloor-engined single-decker, and Mr W.M. Little, then newly-appointed as transport manager, was quick to foresee the advantages of this layout. In 1949-50 three underfloor-engined demonstrators were on trial, being Leyland/MCW HR40 Olympic KOC233 Leyland Royal Tiger/Brush MTC757 and all-Sentinel HAW577. In 1951 three further underfloor-engined single-deckers were obtained, though in ECT livery and bearing fleet numbers, they were actually demonstrators on hire from their makers. 800 (LRW377) was a Daimler Freeline G6H/S with two-door Duple body, while 801 (JFS524) was an Alexander-bodied Royal Tiger and 802 (JFS525) a Leyland/MCW Olympic, both rear-entrance crush-loaders with single seats on the offside. These vehicles entered service on normal single-deck routes, and were mildly success-ful, inasmuch as sixteen all-Leyland Royal Tigers followed in 1952, although with double seats throughout for forty seated passengers and, reputedly, space for fifteen standees. The experimental Daimler was returned to the makers in 1952, and the two Leylands were purchased. In common with several other Edinburgh experimental vehicles, 801 and 802 are now coaches, after conversion in 1954 by their original body-builders. The other Royal Tigers were converted to coaches in 1959-60 by the corporation themselves. Other single-deck demonstrators in this era were Leyland Tiger Cub/Weymann OTD301 and Guy/Saro LJW336.

By 1950 the fate of the Edinburgh tram was in the balance. Although seven second-hand Manchester Corporation 'Pilcher' cars were obtained in 1948, the transport committee were examining the future of this mode of transport. In 1950 tenders had been invited for a new car, and though the lowest tender from an outside builder was over £12,000 (obviously production cars would have been cheaper) the estimated cost of a new Shrubhill-built car was £9,300. On the same subject, Mr Little was invited to Leeds in 1953 to inspect the new railcars just entering service, but declined.

After many years of Daimler/MCW predominance, it was apparent that Mr Little favoured Leylands, and but for the cessation of bus bodybuilding at Leyland, the sixteen Royal Tigers mentioned above and the twentyone all-Leyland

PD2/12s of 1952 might have been the first of many. 1953 produced a very different all-Leyland vehicle in the attractive shape of 185 (FOF298), an ex-Birmingham Corporation TD7 of 1939, with fiftyone-seat body. This vehicle was even more unusual in being fitted with the 0/350 Leyland Comet engine and an AEC preselective gearbox. 185 only lasted two years with ECT. Other unusual deliveries in 1953 were sixty ex-London Transport utility Guy Arabs, widened to 8 ft and fitted with 5LW engines, bearing fiftyfive-seat Duple lightweight bodies. Despite a storm of protests from conservative citizens about Edinburgh buying buses from London – an insult second only to buying buses from Glasgow – these vehicles gave many years of valuable service on tram replacement routes, until relegated to Longstone relief duties, some after more service north of the border than south of it. The only experiments concerning these vehicles have been the substitution of glassfibre roofs on several of the later examples, and the fitment of a two-step rear platform with tramway-style centre pole and rear wall emergency door on 324 in 1957.

The purchase of 300 Leyland PD2 20s with Metro-Cammell Weymann Orion bodies between 1954 and 1957 could hardly be described as an experiment. No one would put these vehicles forward as serious rivals to London's Routemaster as regards interior comfort, but few will deny the great service rendered by them. All but two of the first hundred vehicles (401-500) were sixty-seaters, with rather poor ventilation, but this was later rectified on these vehicles and on further deliveries, 480 and 487 were the prototypes of the second hundred (501-600), and in addition to the increased ventilation, had increased seating capacities. 487 was exhibited at Earls Court in 1954 as a sixtyfour-seater but, like 480, entered service as a sixtythree-seater, setting the trend for 501-600. The third hundred (701-800) followed in 1956-7, and inevitably out of these 300 vehicles, described by a town councillor as 'montrous masses of shivering tin', several have been the subject of experiments. 532, for instance, has a completely glassfibre top-deck, with single-skin roof through-out; 553 was fitted with fluorescent lighting in 1960; 575 was delivered in 1955 unpainted, and ran like this until 1959, as did 781/92-800 of 1957. An experiment of a different type was the loan of 721 to Coras Iompair Eireann in 1957. The remainder of Edinburgh's tram-replacement vehicles were the seventy Guy Arabs with Alexander bodies (901-70) of which only 959 has been subjected to experiment, receiving a Gardner 6LX in 1958 and being repainted in an experimental livery the same year, as is described more fully below.

While the tram replacement vehicles were in the course of delivery, other manufacturers were still offering demonstration vehicles. The Potteries lightweight Daimler CLG5 with proto-type MCW Orion body, H500 (REH500), was tried in 1954 and possibly had a bearing on subsequent deliveries – to the benefit of MCW anyway. Next came 7194H in 1954, the AEC Regent/Park Royal vehicle in City of Oxford colours, and another AEC Regent the next year, 88CMV, in light green, one of the first Regent Vs, also with Park Royal body, 88CMV was tried on services 34/35, where bleary-eyed early-morning Sighthill passengers automatically stood back to let by what was outwardly a Scottish Omnibuses vehicle, and on the 19 Circle, the first of many demonstrators to use this route. During 1956, 30 ft double-deck vehicles on two axles were legalised and the following May, the first such vehicle to operate in Edinburgh, Crossley Bridgemaster 9JML, was tried on the 19 and 34/35. About the same time, orders were placed for two experimental Leyland Titan PD3/2 chassis with fully-automatic gearboxes and seventytwo-seat forward-entrance bodies, one by Alexander and the other by Metropolitan-Cammell. These were to be painted in an experimental black and white livery.

Meantime, replacement of the ageing single-deck fleet was predominant in the minds of the transport committee, and several experiments towards this end were carried out on the No 1 route. The first of these was the trial of the Commer TS3-engined Beadle Chatham demonstrator XKT784 in February 1957, followed in October of that year by TGB-752, the prototype Albion Aberdonian MR11 with fortyone-seat Alexander coach body. About the same time a Tiger Cub from the corporation coach fleet with similar body, 819 (NFS748), was placed in stage service on No 1 route. December 1957 saw the entry into service of ECT 822 (PWS822) an ultralightweight Albion Aberdonian with Alexander fortythree-seat bus body. With the body largely made of glassfibre, the low unladen weight of only 4 tons 12 cwt was achieved. From February to July 1958, the red and ivory colours of UNM606, a Bedford SB8 demonstrator with Leyland 0/350 engine and Duple Midland forty-seat body, could be observed anywhere between Corstophine and Easter Road. For a few days it was joined by a similarly-coloured AEC Reliance demonstrator, PNR891, also with Duple Midland body. After these various experiments, it was decided that the choice of a new standard single-decker lay between three basic types of vehicle – the inexpensive Bedford with short life expectancy; the lightweight underfloor chassis like the Aberdonian; or a double-deck chassis with single-deck body (working on the assumption that most of the Edinburgh lowbridges would soon be removed). After all this, however, the new single-deck fleet materialised as 100 Leyland Tiger Cubs with Weymann bodies.

Aberdonian 822 had made its first public appearance in the demonstration park at the 1957 Scottish Show, but had a more interesting companion inside the Kelvin Hall, 998 (PWS998), the first of the two PD3s, this being the Alexander-bodied example. With Homalloy front, fully-automatic gearbox, front doors, heaters and seventytwo light-blue seats, 998 certainly departed from the standard Edinburgh specification. The light-blue seats combined with a grey-and-white interior scheme were designed to match with the proposed black-and-white exterior which never materialised, possible after experience with these colours on the city coaches.

998 entered service in January 1958 by spending a week on each of the all-day double-deck routes, in depot order. Other double-deck developments at this time included the

appearance of demonstrators SDU711 and 76MME on the 19 Circle, SDU711 was the sixtysix-seat Daimler CVG6 with Willowbrook body, and 76MME, the well-known Bridge-master. The end of 1958 produced another Daimler/Willow-brook demonstrator, this time seventyfour-seater VKV99.

One-man operation came to Edinburgh on 15 June 1958, using three of the 1952 Royal Tigers converted to front-entrance fortythree-seaters. They had manually-operated TIMs. These vehicles were used on service 40 (Portobello-Newcraighill), a short shuttle service necessitated by a low bridge at Jewel Cottages. When these vehicles (810-12) were converted to coaches, three Cubs were used, being replaced eventually by 'real' one-man-operated vehicles, Cubs with electric Setrights and change-giving machines.

Early 1959 produced a number of new vehicles, the first fifty of the Tiger Cubs (1-50) and five more 30 ft Leyland double-deckers (261-4/999). Of the Cubs, 26 was last to arrive, and when it did appear it was found to have fortyseven seats, gaining three seats by using a three-and-two arrangement in three of the rear rows of seats. Four of the 30 ft deckers were synchromesh PD3s with less-luxuriant versions of 998's body, while 999 was the second fully-automatic vehicle ordered at the same time as 998 — although with Alexander body; seemingly the chassis had lain at MCW for some eighteen months before removal to Falkirk. 999's most striking feature, however, was undoubtedly its all-scarlet colour scheme. At about this time, 6LX Guy 959 appeared in an all-cherry red scheme. To add to the spectrum, light blue Walsall Corporation Dennis Loline/Willowbrook 800 (600DDH) appeared on the 19. The Walsall Loline was on loan in exchange for Edinburgh PD3 261, which also saw service with Morecambe Corporation, then all-AEC. Other livery experiments at this time concerned all-Leyland PD2 256 repainted all madder with white waist-band, Leyland PD3 264 repainted with madder covering the lower deck windows and utility Guy 83 partially repainted black-and-white — but never was seen on the streets as such. All of these experiments were carried out with a view to economising by using spray painting methods, but all these vehicles are now repainted in the standard madder and white.

The second fifty Tiger Cubs, 51-100, were delivered between September 1960 and January 1961, and were basically similar to their predecessors, except that they were fortyseven-seaters. 55, exhibited at the 1960 London show, and twenty-four others were fitted with fluorescent lighting. When in October 1960, the 13, hailed by the local press as 'Edinburgh's First One-Man Bus Route' (despite the 40 of 1958 and the 32 of 1959) became one-manned, certain of the newer Cubs were used. Originally fortyseven-seaters, the vehicles used on the 13 eventually lost the two seats behind the driver to make way for a parcel space. No 96 of this batch was fitted with illuminated nearside advertisements in 1961, and some half-dozen similar vehicles are so fitted, all by the corporation.

An interesting batch of demonstrators went into service on the 19 Circle during 1960. First to arrive was 80WMH, the third Bridgemaster demonstrator from AEC. This was followed in a matter of weeks by 661KTJ, the Weymann lowbridge-Atlantean demonstrator. Guy Wulfrunian 7800DA, followed in July that year; the next demonstrator, just under a year later, was the second Wulfrunian, 8072DA.

A very different demonstrator paid a fleeting visit to the city later that summer. With amendment of the length and width regulations imminent (partly through the promptings of Mr Little) a 36 ft Leyland-MCW Olympic vehicle was exhibited to the transport committee. It was one of a consignment of Olympics damaged when the French ammunition ship *La Coubre* blew up in Havana harbour, and on return to Britain for repair it was sent to Edinburgh for this private demonstration. Immediately the 36 ft x 8 ft 2½ in regulations were approved. Edinburgh ordered one of the new Leyland Leopard PSU3 chassis, and the vehicle materialised as the famous 101 (YSG101). This was a standard semi-automatic Leopard, with a definitely non-standard Alexander body, boasting three doors, thirtythree seats, space for thirty standees, large rear platform, space for a seated conductor,

and many other novel refinements. For the five months between its initial showing at the 1961 Scottish Show to its eventual entry into service in April 1962, 101 buzzed back and forwards between Edinburgh, Falkirk and Leyland - even managing a quick trip across to Northern Ireland. It entered service on route 16, receiving the nickname 'Polaris' from its crews, leading a far from uneventful life on this service thereafter. Reporting on its progress to the transport committee in October 1962, Mr Little stated that its average fuel consumption was 8.2 mpg as against 9.6 for a Titan with a similar seating capacity. Despite this, its operating costs were said to be almost the same, and Mr Little disregarded the pleas of an irate councillor who demanded that it be kept in the garage until it could be run more profitably.

Mr Little's ultimate goal was to achieve a complement of 70 to 80 in 101, but in 1963 he was appointed chairman of the Scottish Bus Group, and interest in 101 seemed to wane. It finished working on route 16 in February 1963 and for six months it lay unused until it reappeared on the busy single-deck 1 Circle route, working as a quite uneconomic thirtythree-seated-plus-eight-standing bus. When the bridges on the 1 route were altered and double-deckers substituted in August 1966, 101 transferred to the low-frequency 45 route until taken off service in January 1968 to be converted to an Airport coach in the corporation's Shrubhill works.

Possibly 101 was ahead of its time; if several 101s had been bought and used on the same route, the outcome might have been quite different. As it is, Edinburgh now seems to favour high-capacity double-deckers, and single-deckers are really used only where physically necessary.

In 1962-3 the City Tour coach fleet, composed mainly of converted 1952 Leyland Royal buses, was due for replacement. Bedford VAS1 demonstrator 996FNM was used on tours for a few days in May 1962, and three VAS1s and nine SB5s were ordered for the 1963 season. In March 1963 Bedford VAL14 demonstrator 883HMJ was tried on the 1 Circle route, as tours were not operating by that time. 883HMJ returned in October that year and demonstrated on the Airport service: six VAL14s, three SB5s and one VAS1 were ordered for 1964. The Bedford VAL14 service bus demonstrator 525LMJ also arrived in 1963, and was used on the 1 Circle for a few weeks at the end of the year.

Albion Lowlander LR1 demonstrator 747EUS was a familiar sight on the 19 Circle for several months in 1963. The bus had appeared at the 1961 Scottish Motor Show in Glasgow Corporation colours, and Glasgow used it for some time before it was passed on to Edinburgh for demonstration. Edinburgh painted it in a style close to their standard livery, but it seems the Lowlander had little appeal. An early Lowlander chassis, ordered by Edinburgh Corporation, was sold in 1964 to Western SMT after lying unused in Shrubhill for some time.

With future orders in mind, the new transport manager, Ronald Cox, organised a large-scale demonstration in 1965. Three buses were borrowed, Daimler Fleetline 565CRW, Leyland Atlantean KTD551C and AEC Renown 7552MX, and were used together for four days at a time on three typical city routes. Staff and public comment was invited, and their observations incorporated in the first order for Alexander-bodied Leyland Atlanteans, which materialised in 1965-6 as 801-825. 801 and 802 differ from the remainder of the batch, with their panoramic side windows, and the second batch of Atlanteans, delivered in 1967, all have this feature. The last vehicle in this batch, 900, is a 33ft eightytwo-seater, the first complete 33ft Atlantean to be built, and was exhibited at the 1967 Scottish Motor Show. Newcastle Corporation borrowed 900 for a few days in 1968, in the absence of a proper Leyland demonstrator.

It would appear that the Atlantean will be a suitable standard vehicle for some years to come, and the flow of demonstration vehicles has slowed. One demonstrator in 1967 was Ford R226 coach WEV450F, which was used on the Airport service, and led to Edinburgh's first order for Fords, two R226s for the coach fleet, joined by two further Bedford VALs for the 1968 season.

MANUFACTURERS' DEMONSTRATION VEHICLES IN SERVICE WITH EDINBURGH CORPORATION TRANSPORT SINCE 1945

Registration	Make and type of vehicle	Body builder	Seating capacity
FRW 587	Daimler CVD6	Willowbrook	B35F
FHP 540 (1)	Daimler CVD6	Willowbrook	B35F
ACN 794 (2)	Guy *Arab* 5LW	Guy	B35R
GHP 259 (3)	Daimler CVD6	NCB	H56R
KOC 233	Leyland *Olympic* HR40	MCW	B40F
MTC 757	Leyland *Royal Tiger* PSU1	Brush	B44F
HAW 577	Sentinel STC6	Sentinel	B44F
LRW 377 (4)	Daimler *Freeline* G6H/S	Duple	B36D
JFS 524 (5)	Leyland *Royal Tiger* PSU1/13	Alexander	B31R
JFS 525 (6)	Leyland *Olympic* HR44	MCW	B32R
OTD 301	Leyland *Tiger Cub* PSUC1/1	MCW	B44F
LJW 336	Guy Arab LUF	Saro	B44F
REH 500 (7)	Daimler CLG5	MCW	H58R
7194 H	AEC *Regent III* 9813S	Park Royal	H58R
88 CMV	AEC *Regent V* MD3RV	Park Royal	H61R
XKT 784	Beadle-Commer *Chatham* OE11	Beadle	B45F
9 JML	Crossley *Bridgemaster* B3RA	Crossley	H72R
TGB 752	Albion *Aberdonian* MR11L	Alexander	C41F
SDU 711	Daimler CVG6	Willowbrook	H66R
76 MME	AEC *Bridgemaster* B3RA	Park Royal	H72R
UNM 606	Bedford SB8	Duple Midland	B40F
PNR 891	AEC *Reliance* MU3RV	Duple Midland	B44F
VKV 99	Daimler CVG6LX.30	Willowbrook	H74R
600 DDH (8)	Dennis *Loline* Y2	Willowbrook	H70F
80 WMH	AEC *Bridgemaster* B3RA	Park Royal	H76R
661 KTJ	Leyland *Atlantean* PDR1.1	MCW	L73F
7800 DA	Guy *Wulfrunian* FDW	Roe	H78F
8072 DA	Guy *Wulfrunian* FDW	Roe	H72F
996 FNM	Bedford VAS1	Duple	C29F
883 HMJ	Bedford VAL14	Duple	C52F
747 EUS	Albion *Lowlander*	Alexander	H72F
525 LMJ	Bedford VAL14	Duple Midland	B52F
565 CRW	Daimler *Fleetline* CRG6LX	Alexander	H78F
KTD 551 C	Leyland *Atlantean* PDR1.1	Park Royal	H74F
7552 MX	AEC *Renown* 3B3RA	Park Royal	H71F
WEV 450 F	Ford R226	Plaxton	C52F

Notes: 1 carried fleet number XL1. 2 carried fleet number XL2. 3 carried fleet number DG1. 4 painted in Corporation livery and numbered 800. 5 later purchased by the Corporation and numbered 801. 6 later purchased by the Corporation and numbered 802. 7 was H.500 in the fleet of Potteries Motor Traction Company Ltd. 8 was 800 in the fleet of Walsall Corporation Transport Department.

BUS SERVICES ON THE GREAT NORTH ROAD BETWEEN EDINBURGH AND DONCASTER

J. Graeme Bruce

This paper, which is an extensive study of the operators on one main road, was presented to the Omnibus Society in 1947. Mr Bruce, who is Mechanical Engineer (Lifts and Escalators) for London Transport, proceeds down the high road from Scotland, giving us glimpses of bus and coach history which, taken together, add up to present a microcosm of the history of the industry.

The Great North Road is the longest highway in our country which possesses the essential character of a single road, and has for many generations been in use not merely for local traffic but for journeys spanning the entire distance between the capitals of England and Scotland. The road to an Englishman is the principal artery to Scotland, or at least to Newcastle. To a Scotsman, however, it is the main road to London. A stage coach service between Edinburgh and London is understood to have begun in 1660, and by 1712 was operating at least once a fortnight.

The original Great North Road passed through the city of York, and Dick Turpin must have used it on his famous ride to York; but the road now bearing the official title passes several miles to the west. It is not far from the truth to say that most parts of the road have been in continuous use since Roman days, as ancient towns lie actually upon the old highway, and there are many equally ancient places only a few miles on either side. Many of the oldest coaching inns in the country are to be found along the road. Today it is unrecognisable, being dual tracked for most of its length, at least in England, and by-passing all the towns and villages of any importance.

It was fitting, therefore, that the Ministry of Transport when introducing its route numbering for the main roads of Britain, commenced with this highway, and gave it the designation A1 in the scheme. It is curious, however, that although A1 has been shifted once or twice at several places, to by-pass towns and give a more direct route, north of Newcastle the road is no longer the direct route to Edinburgh.

Turning to the field of road passenger transport, this highway has lost its former glory, when vehicles of various sizes, shapes and hues vied with one another for a place in the stream of traffic. The Road Traffic Act, 1930, has accomplished its primary object, as little now remains except the vehicles of the area or combine companies. In case it should be thought that they have usurped their leading and perhaps final possession of the road, it should be remembered that they too were pioneers of many sections, if not of the whole road from Edinburgh to London.

Most stories about the Great North Road begin at London, but being a Scotsman I propose to reverse this order of things and begin my story in Edinburgh.

Scotland Edinburgh is the capital city of Scotland and can claim to be one of the few cities of beauty in the world. Apart from its historic associations, there are several features of interest to those concerned with transport.

Edinburgh was the scene, so I am told, of the first public regular passenger motor transport service in Britain. The predecessor of Scottish Omnibuses Ltd, namely the Scottish Motor Traction Co Ltd, was itself founded as a passenger motor transport business as early as 14 June 1905. By the following year a number of Maudslay double-deck vehicles were in use on the streets of Edinburgh and by 1914 among many other routes a summer service was being operated along what is now part of the Great North Road to Dunbar.

The SMT Company, owing to the difficulty of obtaining suitable vehicles to come within the Edinburgh police regulations, designed its own, the first one being produced in 1912. The type name, Lothian, was given to the vehicle in consideration of the three counties surrounding Edinburgh. The Lothian was an assembled job and employed the Knight sleeve valve engine similar to that used in the Minerva cars. Even in those days the Edinburgh magistrates approved time-tables and routes and issued licences to operate; all vehicles were passed by a corporation omnibus and hackney carriage inspector; and this was twenty years before the Road Traffic Act! The regulation limiting the length of the vehicle to 23 ft was probably the principal reason for the introduction of the Lothian chassis, which was an early forward control type seating thirtytwo passengers, accommodation which could not be obtained with any type then marketed with a single-deck body.

By 1925, the SMT fleet, wearing a green livery with the letters SMT Co Ltd spread along the waist rail, and charabancs painted a bright yellow, consisted of some 230 single-deckers of which eightyfive were Lothians, most of the others being Maudslays. The all-the-year-round bus route about this time along the Great North Road terminated at Haddington, although a summer service was made to Dunbar. It was not until the railway influence came in 1930 that blue began to be adopted as the fleet colour, and the plain large capital letters SMT used as a fleet name on the sides of the vehicles. In 1948 the livery again returned to green, but of a much brighter shade than previously used, when the title of the company became Scottish Omnibuses Ltd (although the fleet name SMT was retained) upon nationalisation. The use of the fleet name *Scottish Omnibuses* did not begin until 1959, and became *Eastern Scottish* in 1964.

Before leaving 'auld Reekie' (this nickname for Edinburgh is said to originate from the view of the smoke from house chimneys seen from the castle) some mention should be made of the local transport. The needs of the capital are now main-tained by the municipality, which owned until 1952, when the first route was abandoned, an exceedingly fine network of tramways, as well as a considerable motor bus system, which remains. The whole tramway system had been replaced with buses by November 1956.

The Corporation became a transport operator in 1913, when it obtained omnibus powers. No real development took place due to the vehicles being impressed by the War Office. A real start at municipal transport operation was made in 1919 when the 25½ route miles of cable trams operated by the Edinburgh & District Tramways Co were acquired at the termination of the lease.

The corporation had actually purchased all the tramway lines in the city from the original concessionaries between 1896 and 1898, some of which were already operating under cable traction. The Edinburgh & District Tramways Co was formed to operate the system under lease, converting the horse tramways to cable traction. A total of thirtysix route miles was reached under municipal auspices, this being the fourth largest cable system in the world.

Although a cable traction system has many points of recommendation, it has many serious disadvantages. It was said of the Edinburgh system (particularly by the rude commercialised upstarts of Glasgow, who had the finest electric tramway system in the world) that it was quicker to walk when visiting Edinburgh, not because the cable cars were slow but because of the incidence of breakdown. In 1922 electrification commenced, assisted no doubt by the incorporation of the burgh of Leith with Edinburgh which had taken place two years earlier. Leith had converted its horse tramways to electric traction in 1904.

Following on the acquisition of the tramway, the first bus route between Easter Road and Ardmillan Terrace commenced. The bus services do not venture far afield, being all inside the city boundary, as the Scottish Motor Traction, with which cordial relations have existed from an early date, maintain the routes to most outlying districts. Edinburgh has thus been fortunate from the early days, in having a co-ordinated motor bus system, and thus avoiding most of the difficult days of intense competition that were the rule in most other cities. Local bye-laws actually protected the company from excessive competition.

The Great North Road really commences at the end of Princes Street, perhaps the most famous street in Britain next to Piccadilly, although the latter name is now more associated with an underground station than a thoroughfare. For several years a subsidiary of the National Electric Construction Co, the Musselburgh & District Electric Light & Traction Co Ltd, operated trams (and later buses) from the GPO at the end of Princes Street to Port Seton, the principal part of the route lying along the Great North Road. The Musselburgh company had constructed and operated an electric tramway between Joppa and Port Seton in 1905, the through service to Edinburgh being made in 1923. The company began operating buses in 1928 over the same route using the fleet name Coast Line, three years later selling most of the tramway undertaking to the Edinburgh municipal authorities. The bus service continued its existence until 1936 when it was acquired by the SMT.

June 1928, saw the introduction of the first through route to England by SMT – a service to Newcastle, but via Jedburgh. It was a month later before the Great North Road was used by a joint service with the United company, following upon the acquisition of a service pioneered by Amos Proud & Sons in 1927. A service was inaugurated by SMT to London in April 1930, and thus the road was covered completely.

In the season of 1928 Edinburgh was linked with Newcastle by four different routes worked by nine different operators. Most of these concerns will be mentioned in the course of the paper but certain services are not seen again on the journey south. An interesting service was that maintained until 1933 between Newcastle and Aberdeen by Thomas Allen & Sons of Blyth. The route taken, however, was not by the Great North Road, but via Kelso. Services local to Blyth were established by this concern in 1910, but its independent existence was lost by United acquisition in 1933, the through service to Aberdeen being withdrawn. This firm also operated a Newcastle − London service in the 1928-9 period with Leyland vehicles. Connections were later provided by Phillipsons.

Another service operated over the Kelso road until 1933 was that by County Motor Services Ltd, a company which should not be confused with the one-time subsidiary of Northern General, the General County Omnibus Co Ltd. The former company came into existence in 1929 to acquire the omnibus business of Gordon & Sons of Choppington, Northumberland, which had begun operating long distance services in 1929. A service between Glasgow and London was still advertised in 1932, but the company is more generally remembered for its Glasgow to Whitley Bay service. This long distance service was acquired jointly by United and SMT and withdrawn about the 1933 season. The Azure Blue luxury Daimler vehicles provided in 1930 and for subsequent seasons a two-day journey to Edinburgh and a three-day journey to Inverness by both East and West coasts.

Returning to the Great North Road, England is entered about three miles north of Berwick-on-Tweed at the Lamberton Toll House where marriages were performed similar in romantic notoriety to the Gretna Green affairs. The toll-house keeper used to exhibit a notice bearing the inscription 'ginger beer sold here and marriages performed.'

Berwick is a town which has had a chequered career, especially in the days of open warfare between Scotland and England. Ownership of the town was disputed, and for about 300 years it remained neutral, being attached to Northumberland for local government purposes comparatively recently. The provision of this buffer state in olden times caused it to become the refuge of undesirables. A new road bridge has been constructed across the Tweed at Berwick, but the main road used to pass over the old narrow many arched bridge of historic interest, which has been preserved. Having crossed the Tweed the territory of United Automobile Services Ltd, and England proper, is entered.

Northern England United began its life a long way off the

Great North Road at Lowestoft in the spring of 1912. In the autumn of the same year a branch was established at Bishop Auckland, only a short distance off the road, in County Durham. In 1920 another branch was opened at Blyth, in Northumberland and soon services embraced Morpeth which is astride the highway. United opened a further branch at Ripon in 1922, which also gave access to the Great North Road.

The company was thus operating after the 1914-18 war in four distinct areas of which three embraced parts of the Great North Road. The vehicles were painted yellow, prior to the acquisition of the organisation jointly by Tilling and British Automobile Traction and the LNER in 1929, after which the now familiar red livery was finally adopted. United, after becoming a combine company, entered into a period of rationalisation, whereby the southernmost parts were transferred to the Lincolnshire and Eastern Counties companies. The area of operation of the company is, however, still split for all intents and purposes in two parts, there being a portion in Northumberland and a portion in Durham and North Yorkshire, the territory in between being served by the Northern General group of companies. Even different trade unions represent the operating staffs in the two areas.

The Great North Road now passes through the county town of Alnwick. United strengthened its hold on the road in 1932 by the acquisition of Rutherfords Coaches working between Alnwick and Berwick. John Lee and Sons' Thropton to Newcastle service which traversed the Great North Road for most of its journey also passed to United. A wonderful view of Alnwick Castle, the seat of the Duke of Northumberland, which has been in the possession of the Percy family since the 15th century, is seen from the Lion Bridge. The castle was once the principal bastion against the Scots invaders, a peril which still remains but against which the castle is no longer adequate protection — and so, on towards Newcastle. William Rufus built the new castle and the Roman name of Monkchester fell into disuse for the town surrounding the castle.

The Newcastle Corporation tramways system was formerly met just north of East Brunton, where the tracks came out of Gosforth Park. A private right of way light railway was operated in the precincts of the Park. Newcastle was granted powers for the operation of tramways, which had been constructed by the municipality, in 1892, being among the first local authorities to receive such powers. An extensive tramway network was built up and in 1927 powers were obtained for the conversion to motor bus operation, but little change took place. In 1935 however, additional powers were received for trolleybus conversions, and a considerable number of the tramway routes were converted to this form of traction. The trolleybus system however was in its final death throes by 1968, giving way to the motor bus.

Newcastle Corporation commenced operating motor buses in 1912, obtaining powers two years later for a route to Long Benton, outside the municipal boundary to the north and just east of the Great North Road. This route was the beginning of a considerable system extending in many cases a long way beyond the city limits.

Newcastle Corporation motors were for long known locally as 'the blue buses', to contrast with the Northern General and United shades of red. The corporation trams were mainly brown in colour, but the trolleybuses were painted a bright yellow, which later became the motor bus fleet colour also.

The Tyne provides a formidable barrier at Newcastle due to the steep approaches at both sides. The High Level Bridge was opened in September 1849, carrying a railway on the top deck and a street below. The bridge was a toll one until recent times, at a charge of ½d for each pedestrian and 4d for cars; horse buses, however, were allowed to use the bridge at a charge of ½d per wheel, and a private firm operated such a service until about 1930, although electric trams commenced to use the bridge in January 1923. The highway was only wide enough to take the double tram track and is principally used by single-deck vehicles, although double-deckers of restricted clearance can and do use it. A new bridge, known as the New Tyne Bridge, was officially opened in 1929, over which most of the traffic passes.

Newcastle lies on the north bank of the river; once across the bridges the town of Gateshead is entered. A company was formed in 1880 to operate tramways in Gateshead and Felling entitled the Gateshead & District Tramways Co and a tramway was constructed along the Great North Road to Low Fell. Considerable extensions took place and inter-running with Newcastle Corporation was established across both bridges. The Gateshead company was the largest company-owned and operated system of tramways to survive the second world war unconverted to motor bus operation. The Gateshead council from time to time sought powers of acquisition, but because of being in a Special Area, in receipt of financial assistance, it was never successful. The company obtained powers for converting the system to trolleybus working so that through connection with Newcastle should not be broken, but replacement was eventually made with motor buses.

The Gateshead tramways were electrified in 1901, an extension from Low Fell to Chester-le-Street along the Great North Road being mooted, but by 1913, the motor bus having passed the experimental stage, a Straker Squire double-decker was acquired to provide this extension. Soon some eight vehicles were being run by the tramway company from the tramway terminus. In 1913 a new company was formed by the BET organisation, which controlled Gateshead Tramways, to acquire these buses. Thus the now famous Northern General Transport Co Ltd, with headquarters at Chester-le-Street, was born. The only serious competition between Gateshead and Chester-le-Street was terminated in 1924 by the acquisition of the Crescent buses. The Gateshead & District company is now a subsidiary of its own offspring. It formerly worked the parcels carrying business in the area for both companies with motor vehicles, although at that time owning no motorbuses; it was the second BET associated concern to begin a parcels carrying business.

Chester-le-Street, the headquarters of Northern General, is

today by-passed, but the Great North Road used to pass through this mining town of ancient origin, which possesses a number of historic buildings as well as evidence of Roman occupation. The next centre of importance is Durham, but there the Great North Road passes about half-a-mile to the west at Neville's Cross. Durham is a city which is very old and, even to those little interested in historic buildings, of considerable beauty. Its charter has been held since 1179.

At Durham the territory of Northern General ends and the southern area of United is encountered. Durham was the scene of motor bus operation by the old Northern Eastern Railway under road powers originally obtained in 1871, with further coverage by an Act of 1905. These powers were naturally passed on to the LNER, the services being continued by the railway until the 1928 Act provided the means of consolidation with the United and Northern General companies. A railway bus route traversed the Great North Road for a short distance from Durham on the way to Sacriston through a mining township with the heartrending name of Pity Me. The transfer of the routes to the area companies, most of them to United, took place about 1930.

County Durham and the North Riding of Yorkshire have been, and to a lesser extent still are provided with road transport connections by independent operators. Many of these have naturally fallen by the wayside, mostly absorbed by the big operators. One was the General County Omnibus Co Ltd, formed in 1927 to acquire the services established by J.A. Kay and to amalgamate those of certain other operators. This company worked a trunk route from Newcastle to Middlesbrough using the Great North Road as far as Durham. Northern General acquired a large financial interest in it in 1930, but continued to operate it as a separate organisation (using Northern General livery) until 1936, when absorption took place, United becoming responsible for the Durham – Middlesbrough section of the route.

Between Durham and Darlington on the Great North Road lies the township of Ferryhill, the home of a number of

independent operators, both past and present. The business
of Walters & Johnson, established at this point by Walters as
early as 1920 and working a service between Darlington and
Durham was acquired by the United in 1932.

The ABC Motor Service which operated a route between
Darlington and Sunderland, using the Great North Road as
far as Ferryhill also had its headquarters there. This service
was a co-operative affair, the ABC in the title standing for the
three members of the syndicate, J. Aaron & Sons, R. Binks,
and P.J. Coulson & Son, who each provided a certain number
of vehicles, the livery generally being green. P.J. Coulson &
Son later retired from the fray.

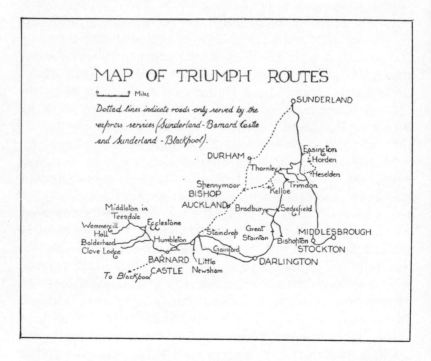

(Fig 1) *Darlington Triumph* motor bus routes from Omnibus Society
archives. One of the biggest independents in Durham, D.T. Todd's
Darlington Triumph company was bought in 1950 by the British
Transport Commission and became part of the new *Durham District*
company, now in its turn wound up

Darlington, besides being the present headquarters of the United Automobile Company, was also the base for one of the largest independents in the area, David Todd, who traded as Darlington Triumph Services. Regular services of this company were not however maintained along the Great North Road. The business was merged in 1951 with ABC and Express Services of Durham to form Durham District Services, a subsidiary of United. This concern continued its separate existence until 1968, when United absorbed its services and vehicles.

Another existing independent service which traverses the Great North Road from Newcastle to a point south of Durham where it branches off to Spennymoor and Bishop Auckland is that known as the OK Motor Services. The principal partner in this syndicate is R. Emmerson of Bishop Auckland, but until 1968 E. Howe of Spennymoor jointly worked the Newcastle service, while other operators 'have shared in the working of routes centred on Bishop Auckland, trading under the general title of OK Motor Services and using a similar reddish-brown livery.

The municipal services of Darlington are met at Harrowgate Hill, about two miles from the town centre. This route was operated as a tramway until about 1926 when conversion of the Darlington system to trolleybuses began. An experimental bus service was tried by Darlington Corporation in 1927 with two Dennis vehicles which it is understood were hired for the purpose. This service only lasted a very short time, since when Darlington has operated single-deck trolleybuses only. In 1947 proposals were made for the operation of both double-deck trolleybuses and of motor buses, but the decision was taken to abandon the trolleybuses, and this process was completed finally in 1957, the first motor buses being placed in service in 1950. The change from an all trolleybus policy may date from 1937, when the transport system ceased to be part of the Electricity Department and became a department on its own account.

The 'natural' or old Great North Road passes out of

Darlington due south to Northallerton, Thirsk and York, but the modern or commercial Great North Road turns westward to Scotch Corner before turning southwards, and does not join up with the old road until Doncaster is reached. The local services on the old road out of Darlington were first worked by two independent operators, although the United operated a through service to Northallerton over the same route. The two operators concerned were James and Mosley (trading as the Croft Motor Services) and Wm Abbott & Sons. The latter worked a service to Dalton on the main road, while the former had a small number of routes with Croft Spa as the principal centre. Both have been absorbed by United.

Yorkshire The A1 is covered by United for local services, and is used by most of the long distance routes out of Darlington to the south. It is in United territory until Boroughbridge is reached, when the area of the West Yorkshire Road Car Co Ltd is entered. The road between Baldersby Gate and Boroughbridge is not covered by a stage service of the area companies as most routes divert via Ripon.

The West Yorkshire company commenced operation in 1906 as the Harrogate Road Car Co Ltd, with a fleet of Clarkson steam buses on local services. By 1924, when Tilling and BAT acquired a controlling interest, the services had spread so that the Great North Road was reached at Wetherby and Boroughbridge. The name of the company was changed at this time to the Harrogate & District Road Car Co and in 1928, when the company became a public one, today's familiar title was adopted.

The West Yorkshire company is perhaps of particular interest because of its special associations with two municipalities. At Keighley in 1932 an agreement was reached between the company and the local corporation for the operation of joint services. In this case a separate company was formed entitled Keighley-West Yorkshire Services Ltd, which is provided with assets of equal value from each undertaking, and the fifty-fifty basis is continued for all new capital expenditure; the day-to-day management of the undertaking

being under the control of West Yorkshire.

At York (where we are more concerned, as the town is situated on the old North Road), the corporation operated tramways, trolleybuses and buses. Agreement was reached in 1933 with West Yorkshire for a similar arrangement to that working at Keighley, except that the new company should own as well as control the assets provided, shares being issued to each of the parties to the agreement. York Corporation promoted a Bill to legalise this procedure, as normally a municipality is not entitled to hold shares in a trading concern. The Bill did not, however, pass the committee stage of the Commons and a new agreement had to be made. The York-West Yorkshire Joint Committee was therefore formed, each party providing the assets in equal proportions, the services operated being under the management of the company.

The tramway service at York was completely abandoned in 1933 after a year's operation under the auspices of the joint committee. The trams were old-fashioned open top four-wheel vehicles working on a 3 ft 6 in gauge track in narrow streets, and the residents were not sorry to see them replaced. Bus and trolleybus powers were obtained in 1914. A short trolleybus service was inaugurated in 1920, ceased to operate in 1929 but was re-opened again in 1931 for a few years.

For long a distinctive feature of many of the West Yorkshire vehicles was the use of a destination board instead of a blind, fitted into a frame erected on the roof of single-deck types.

The situation immediately south of the West Yorkshire company's official area is confused as far as federated operators are concerned, as it is not until Doncaster is approached that the stage carriage vehicles of the Yorkshire Traction Company are seen, the next combine company on the journey south.

Before this company's area is reached, however, the territory of the West Riding Automobile Co Ltd, is traversed. Although West Riding was never directly associated with the railway companies, it is an area agreement company. It was originally incorporated as a tramway company with the title Yorkshire (West Riding) Electric Tramways Co Ltd, in 1905; with tramway services based on Wakefield, and a separate system in Pontefract. A subsidiary, the West Riding Automobile Company was formed to operate bus services in 1922. The parent absorbed the subsidiary company in 1935, when the trams were abandoned, and changed its name to that previously used by the subsidiary.

Little West Riding operation takes place along the Great North Road, but several routes cross at various points to reach such centres as Knottingley, Monk Fryston and Selby from Leeds, Wakefield and Pontefract. The West Riding company uses a pleasant green colour scheme for most vehicles, but those engaged on working old tramway routes, on which certain cheaper fares are available, are painted what might be termed 'combine' red.

The territory of the West Riding concern has been invaded by a number of independent operators. J. Bullock & Sons commenced operation as motor bus proprietors in 1913. In 1928 the partnership became a limited liability company with a similar title, having headquarters at Featherstone, Yorkshire, only a short distance off the Great North Road. B&S buses (to use the company's fleet name) only traversed the Great North Road on regular stage carriage services for a short distance between Brotherton and Ferrybridge, although other routes crossed it at several points and in addition the Great North Road was used as an entry into Doncaster. J. Bullock & Sons, one of the largest independent operators in Britain, owning over 150 vehicles and working some thirty stage carriage routes in the West Riding of Yorkshire, lost its independent existence in 1950, being acquired by the West Riding Automobile Company.

Another branch of the Bullock family formed South Yorkshire Motors Ltd, in 1930 to take over some existing services. A number of stage carriage routes is operated in the same territory.

At Woodlands, near Adwick-le-Street and only 4½ miles north of Doncaster, the stage carriage buses of the Yorkshire Traction company are encountered. This company commenced business a few miles to the west of the Great North Road as the Barnsley & District Electric Traction Company Ltd, in 1902, as a subsidiary of the BET group formed to operate tramways and light railways. The 'electric' in the title was dropped in 1919, as the bus services commenced in 1913 had outstripped the tramways, which were confined to some short routes in Barnsley. The name of the company was again changed in 1928 to the Yorkshire Traction Co Ltd, just prior to the acquisition of shares by the LMS and LNE Railways equal to the BET holding. Services into Doncaster were established at an early date and a number of joint services is now worked with Doncaster Corporation.

Doncaster is famous for three things: the St Leger, butterscotch, and as a railway centre. In the field of passenger transport it is no less famous. Doncaster Corporation tramways, which began operating in 1902, were met with at Woodlands, from where the private reserved track ran alongside the Great North Road for several miles into Doncaster. The system itself was unusual in that a centre-grooved rail and wheels with a double tread were used. Abandonment of the tramways began in 1925 and was completed by 1935, being replaced mainly by trolleybuses. The first trolleybus route was opened in 1928 to replace the tramway to Bentley which ran out of Doncaster for a short distance along the old Great North Road before branching east. The first motor bus service inaugurated by Doncaster Corporation, in 1922, was also operated along the Great North Road as far as Adwick-le-Street, a route which is now jointly operated with Yorkshire Traction. Trolleybus abandonment began in 1961, although the Bentley route was changed over to buses as early as 1956. Trolleybuses were finally withdrawn in December 1963.

Long Distance Services So far little has been said about long distance services on the Great North Road, which in the early days passed through many stages. Long distance motor coach operation can be said to have commenced, at least as far as the Great North Road is concerned, when Orange Bros of Bedlington, Northumberland, began a once-weekly service from Newcastle to London in June 1927. This service quickly developed into a twice-weekly one, and very soon was being operated twice daily. The venture was so successful that Orange Bros gave up operating local bus services to concentrate on their long distance activities. Perhaps this was a mistake, as several years later they again became local operators by acquiring the Morpeth-Bedlington service of Kanes Motors early in 1933. Orange Bros extended one day and one night working to Edinburgh and Glasgow, via the Great North Road in both England and Scotland, after having, from the winter of 1928, advertised connection at Newcastle with the SMT/United services to and from Edinburgh and Glasgow.

Majestic Saloon Coaches (Robert Armstrong & Sons of Ebchester) followed very shortly on the Orange lead with a Newcastle-London service, also along the Great North Road. For a short time Majestic operated through to Edinburgh and Glasgow. The original Majestic vehicles were mainly Gilfords. Services quickly followed by Glenton Friars, Charltons, Phillipsons and National Coachways.

National Coachways succeeded to the route inaugurated by a concern based on Chester-le-Street with the name of Cestrian, which from the summer of 1929 operated for a short time from Glasgow to London via Edinburgh and Newcastle and, early in 1930, introduced a London-Middlesbrough-Sunderland-West Hartlepool-Newcastle service. The service between Glasgow and Newcastle was withdrawn in December 1931, as a licence was not granted by the Northern Traffic Commissioners; the service between Newcastle and London via the coast road however, received sanction.

National Coachways became associated in 1930 with Glenton Friars (Road Coaches) Ltd, a company incorporated in 1928 to acquire the services commenced in 1927 by Mr Friar of Blaydon-on-Tyne and known as the North Road Coach Services. The dusty grey, blue lined Glenton Friar Daimler vehicles set a fine example in luxury coach travel with rear facing back seat and kitchenette. Later Glenton Friars vehicles were the first observation coaches used in regular service, at least on the Great North Road, if not in Britain. The Glenton Friars service operated directly along the Great North Road while the National Coachway vehicles, also luxurious Daimlers, operated via the coast, joining the Great North Road on the southward journey at Doncaster.

Another proprietor, F. Taylor of Middlesbrough, working under the title of Blue Band Bus Service, operated a London service from Middlesbrough, later extended to Sunderland, which commenced in 1927. A night service, introduced in 1929, did not at first work through Middlesbrough but gave connections therefore at Stockton. United acquired this operator in 1930, beginning its encroachment into what had been an independent's paradise. United extended the service into Newcastle. The Sunderland-Middlesbrough-London route was also covered in the 1928-9 period by coaches bearing the fleet name 'Overoads' (which were operated originally by Wray's Garage, of Pity Me, via Stockton, York and Tadcaster), and by vehicles bearing the fleet name Broadway. This latter service south of Doncaster deviated by way of Nottingham, Leicester and Northampton.

In 1932 United acquired Glenton Friars and National Coachways completely as well as a substantial shareholding in Majestic Saloon Coaches (London and Newcastle) Ltd. The Glenton Friars and National Coachways vehicles appeared with their familiar fleet names but United colours for one season only — then oblivion. Majestic continued to operate as a separate entity until the winter of 1936, when this name too disappeared.

J. Charlton & Sons of Hebburn-on-Tyne operated under the fleet name of 'Blue Safety Coaches' a service between Newcastle and London via the Great North Road entirely, until the 1931 season when the route was changed north of Durham to include Sunderland and South Shields. A Sunderland-London service via Middlesbrough and York was also operated for a time, and a local service between Hebburn and South Shields. The United acquired Charltons in 1935, this famous

name, the last non-combine one, disappearing shortly afterwards.

Phillipson Stella Motor Services Ltd, another early operator,
seemed to originate at the London end of the road, the route
covered being in the first place the direct one along the Great
North Road. A service was also worked from London to
Scarborough. In 1933 this company came into the United
fold, but continued to operate for several years as a separate
entity with a slight re-arrangement of route.

Orange Bros was acquired by Thos Tilling Ltd in 1933, and
a new company constituted, the services then being co-
ordinated with United (also a Tilling associated concern since
1929, when Tilling and BAT had acquired shares). This
co-ordination with United cleared up an anomalous situation
which had arisen for London Coastal Coaches, who had
booked for Orange Bros from the early days, and had also to
accept United when they entered the arena in 1930. For over
three years, therefore, Coastal had been terminal agents for
two directly competing services. For licensing reasons, Orange
Bros remained as a separate firm, controlled by United, for a
number of years, and the colour scheme of the present-day
United coaches is derived from this association with Orange
Bros. The operation of the London-Scotland services of
Orange were withdrawn in favour of the SMT services upon
co-ordination with United.

Thus in the season of 1935 the United operating group
consisted of Orange working a direct service to Newcastle and
one via Darlington, Durham, Sunderland and South Shields;
Phillipson working one via Darlington and Bishop Auckland
and one via Durham, Sunderland and South Shields; Majestic
working a direct service to Newcastle; and United itself
working via York, Stockton, West Hartlepool and Sunderland. The Traffic Commissioners were anxious to reduce the
number of vehicles operating on the Great North Road,
particularly the Newcastle services. United was therefore
compelled to retain the subsidiary companies or possibly
lose the timings altogether. Phillipson's services were actually

suspended on a duplication technicality and thereafter disappeared.

Two other operators working London-Newcastle services were the Tyne & Thames Motor Coach Service (which provided the 'Nite' Motor Coach service, using vehicles with reclining chairs, on a thrice-weekly service routed via Doncaster, York and Darlington), and the Minerva Saloon Service routed over the modern Great North Road. The Minerva service worked under various ownerships, including City Bus Service, British Road Services Ltd, and the Ideal Bus Service Company, and began as a South Shields-Newcastle-London service. The exact dates of disappearance into the United fold are obscure. Another operator whose exact workings are now lost by the passage of time was the General Pullman Motor Services of Newcastle, which advertised a daily service from Newcastle to London via the Great North Road through York in 1928. This is not to be confused with the South Shields-Newcastle-Darlington-London service of General County Motor Services initiated about the same time.

E. Thomson (subsequently Thomson Tours Ltd), operated a twice-weekly London-Edinburgh service as early as 1928, with one journey via Chester and one via York each week. The journey took two days. It was later proposed to work double-deck luxury sleeping coaches on the routes, after operation via Chester had been abandoned, but the proposals did not meet with the traffic commissioners' approval. The idea was not followed up as the concern was acquired by SMT in 1930.

In the autumn of 1928 some sleeper coaches constructed on Guy six-wheel chassis were introduced on a thrice-weekly Newcastle-London service on the Great North Road by a Darlington firm, Express Motors. These coaches, which were single-deck vehicles, had twelve bunks. The innovation seems to have been unsatisfactory, as the service faded out with little trace, although the local bus services of Eastern Express continued, to be taken over by LNER. Its operations from

London were known as Varsity Express.

The first Glasgow-London connection, it is believed, was given by Clan Motorways via Newcastle. The Clan service was between Glasgow and Newcastle, extended later to Whitley Bay, but the route taken was via Carlisle and therefore, strictly speaking, lies outside the scope of this paper. Connection was made at Newcastle with the Majestic service and through bookings were taken, but two days were required for the journey. By 1929, however, Clan had re-routed its service via Peebles, Melrose and Jedburgh.

Midland Bus Services of Glasgow commenced the first direct through London service via Carlisle and Scotch Corner to the Great North Road. In February 1929 SMT obtained control of the Midland, converting Mr Sword's concern into Midland Bus Services Ltd, and the crimson-red vehicles became blue. In 1938 a rationalisation of the bus industry in Scotland took place, and the Midland became part of Western SMT. The confusion which existed in London Coastal booking office, due to there being two red 'Midland' companies, was alleged to be great, and stories are told of dear old ladies arriving in Glasgow and asking the way to Smethwick. Even the change in livery did not avoid confusion, as a large proportion of British people seemed to be colour blind.

There are many other long distance services which use the Great North Road in addition to those working London to Newcastle or to Scotland. The West Yorkshire company commenced in July 1929 a Harrogate-London service which used the road for most of the way. This service was the beginning of the Yorkshire Pool, as the following year Yorkshire Traction and Yorkshire (Woollen District) joined West Yorkshire in providing a co-ordinated network of long distance routes between Yorkshire and London and the Midlands. The following routes were then operated:

Harrogate-London, via Great North Road;
Bradford-London, via Midlands;
Keighley-Birmingham, via Barnsley and Sheffield;
Harrogate-Birmingham, via Doncaster and Nottingham.

There were three independent operators working services to Leeds from London at this time. Two used part of the Great North Road; South Yorkshire Motors as far as Doncaster, and Wilks Parlour Car Services as far as Grantham; a third, B & E Motor Services, ran by way of the Midlands. The latter firm had its headquarters in Doncaster, and operated a local service from there to Skellow, a village to the east of the Great North Road. The three services were co-ordinated in 1932 under the title of London, Midland & Yorkshire Services Ltd, and the Halifax to London service continued to use the Great North Road. The group was acquired by the Yorkshire Pool in 1935. Another independent London-Leeds service via the Great North Road was that maintained by the Hale Garage and Coach Company & Coachways Ltd. Yorkshire Pool took over these operations in 1933. Coachways Ltd also operated a London-Hull service.

East Yorkshire joined the Yorkshire Pool in 1931, although they had been operating a London service from Scarborough via Bridlington and Barnsley with a feeder from Hull to Barnsley since the summer of 1929, in competition with the Phillipson service. Phillipson's Scarborough service was transferred to the Yorkshire Pool in 1935.

East Midland Motor Services Ltd joined the Yorkshire Pool in 1933 when the Sheffield service which used the Great North Road only as far as Hitchin was added to the Pool. This service was inaugurated by Underwood Express Services Ltd, a predecessor of East Midland.

What other long distance services have used the Great North Road? Probably the most famous of all is the Limited Stop Pool. A service was commenced on 1 May 1928 by the Northern General Transport Co Ltd from Newcastle to Liverpool via Leeds and Manchester, with charabanc type vehicles making one journey per day in each direction. On 15 May of the following year the West Yorkshire, Yorkshire (Woollen District) and North Western companies joined Northern in operating the service on a two-hour frequency. The East Yorkshire company began a service between Hull and Manchester about the same time, and in February 1930 joined the Pool. In 1932, when the Lancashire United company also joined, an hourly frequency was maintained (every two hours via Altrincham, the original route, and every two hours via Eccles). This service only used the Great North Road from Newcastle to Baldersby Gate, the cross roads for Ripon. A competitive service, Tyne & Mersey Motor Services Ltd of Gateshead, registered in 1930 and latterly associated with Thomas Allen & Co of Blyth, was acquired on behalf of the Pool in 1933. This service took in Bradford, and one of the Limited Stop journeys was diverted daily to cover this point after acquisition.

The Fawdon Bus Co Ltd, a Newcastle firm, registered in 1927, commenced a service from Newcastle to Birmingham, later extended to Coventry, using the Great North Road as far as Wetherby. In 1933 this concern was acquired by Northern General on behalf of a Limited Stop Pool, but was continued as a separate concern in view of the fact that more than half of the service overlapped into the Yorkshire Pool area. The Newcastle-Leeds section was taken over by the Limited Stop Pool and the Leeds-Coventry section by the Yorkshire Pool. The Fawdon Bus company, however, continued to exist as a joint subsidiary of all the firms interested in the two pools for many years, although no vehicles were latterly owned by the concern. Another company, the Great North of England Omnibus Co Ltd, worked a service from Newcastle to Notting-ham partly over the Great North Road. This route was acquired by the big group but the company still flourishes with a Darlington-Carlisle service.

United purchased in August 1933 the Leeds & Newcastle Omnibus Co Ltd, a company registered in 1927 with head-quarters at Northallerton. Two services were operated, one using part of the Great North Road between the cities in its title; and the other running from Leeds to Middlesbrough and Sunderland, which crossed the Great North Road at Baldersby Gate. Following this purchase, on 9 December 1934, United was included in the Limited Stop Pool. East Yorkshire with-drew its Hull service at this time, a Middlesbrough branch (extended to Redcar in the summer) being substituted.

The Limited Stop Service was then consolidated as follows:

(1)   A two-hourly Liverpool - Newcastle service via Altrincham - Dewsbury - Leeds;

(2)   A two-hourly Liverpool - Middlesbrough (Redcar in summer) service via Eccles - Liversedge - Leeds;

(3)   One return journey daily between Liverpool and Newcastle via Eccles - Bradford - Leeds;

(4)   One return journey daily between Newcastle and Coventry via Wetherby - Leeds.

Another firm, operating as Overland Motor Services, worked between Middlesbrough and Liverpool about 1929, but was later acquired by the Tyne & Mersey company, who co-ordinated it with their Newcastle-Liverpool service while retaining the *Overland* fleet name. MacShane's Motors Ltd also operated between Liverpool and Newcastle, but via Carlisle, and between Liverpool and Middlesbrough via Leeds and York (neither service running on the Great North Road for any distance), about the same period.

In the summer of 1929 the East Midland and United Automobile companies worked a Retford-Doncaster-York-Thirsk-Darlington-Newcastle service, which was numbered twenty-six by both operators. It did not reappear in subsequent years. A service was also operated from Redcar to Leeds via Northallerton by Redwing Safety Services, a business formed in 1925. This operated for a time via Darlington and the Great North Road, but the shorter route was adopted later. In February 1929 the LNER obtained a substantial interest in this concern, a new company, Redwing Safety Services Ltd, being formed. United absorbed Redwing in 1933. A Leeds-Middlesbrough service had, however, been jointly operated by United and West Yorkshire from 31 August 1932.

Another similar service in this area was that commenced by J. Smith of Middlesbrough in 1927 using the fleet name *Safety*. Local services were also worked, and in addition one to Newcastle via Durham and the Great North Road, with journeys extended to Edinburgh and Glasgow, in the 1928-9 period. United obtained an interest in the concern in 1930, forming a limited liability company to acquire the assets and operate the local services, the Newcastle-Scotland service being withdrawn.

G. Galley of Newcastle, under the operating title of Galleys Express Motors, commenced a service between Newcastle and York in 1928, extending it to Hull in 1930, but after the traffic commissioners got busy, an all-the-year-round licence was only granted to York, the Hull service being deemed seasonal. This service made use of the Great North Road between Newcastle and Darlington and was still operating in 1939, but has since been acquired by East Yorkshire.

We have had a brief glimpse into the past glories of the Great North Road. What of the future? The days of cut throat competition are gone for ever, and undoubtedly the transport worker has benefited in better conditions and higher wages; the spice of variety has gone, however, and the trend appears to be the complete submersion of all individuality in one gigantic undertaking, one make, one colour, one ticket and one uniform.

MY FIRST SEVENTEEN YEARS OF MANAGEMENT

Norman H. Dean

Sub-titled The Origins of Hebble, *this paper was presented to the Omnibus Society in 1959, when Mr Dean was General Manager of the Yorkshire Traction Company Ltd. It can be read as the story of an individual operator, but its great value is the insight it gives into operating conditions in the years before the Road Traffic Act 1930 came into effect, and into the negotiations between the various interests concerned in the settlement of the industry at that time. Mr Dean became President of the Society in 1964.*

I think it is true to say that most managers of Bus Undertakings reach their position by promotion from the Traffic or Engineering Departments. A few start from the lowest rungs of the traffic or engineering ladders, and all credit is due to such who reach managership as a result of real hard work, determination and ability.

I started in a different way, for the position of traffic manager of a small bus undertaking of five vehicles was thrust upon me at a time when I had no stage carriage experience whatever, having only a limited knowledge of private hire and excursion work, but a fair engineering knowledge of commercial vehicles.

For the most part my paper is the story of the Hebble Company from its commencement in December, 1924 to the end of May, 1939, when I left to take up my subsequent position with the Yorkshire Traction Company. However, as the Hebble Company would never have come into being except for certain events which took place before December,

1924, I consider it necessary to briefly chronicle my early experience in transport.

I left school in July, 1914, at the age of 14, after spending three years at a Secondary School in Halifax, the town in which I was born and bred. I left school because I wanted to do so and there was no objection from my parents. However, I subsequently attended Halifax Technical College three nights per week for an engineering course.

My father and two uncles (Oliver and Charles Holdsworth) were equal partners in a business founded by my grandfather in 1870. They had about twentyfour horses for the main business of general carriers and removal contractors but in addition supplied up to 500 horses each summer for Army Training Camps, most of the horses being purchased in Ireland in the spring and then sold the following September. However, the mechanisation of the Army during the 1914-18 war put an end to this section of the business.

I started to work in the family business and actually never had thoughts of doing anything else. By 1915 the firm was operating Garrett and Foden steam wagons, on which vehicles I quite often acted as steersman, no licences being required in those days. I also did a considerable amount of furniture removing, and by the age of 16 was able to do the skilled job of packing van loads of furniture. In 1916 the firm purchased a 3½ ton British Berna and the following year a 5 ton Swiss Berna. As soon as I was able to obtain a driving licence at 17 I started regularly to drive motor lorries and occasionally the steam wagons on all types of haulage work, until I was called up on reaching the age of 18.

My father died in May, 1918 and mother, no doubt being rather concerned at the adventuresome spirit of her brothers, decided to withdraw her financial interest in the business. However, as a result of this, my prospects of being an eventual participant in the business diminished considerably.

I was demobilised in December, 1918 and went straight back to my old job. For a couple of years I continued chiefly with haulage work, driving vehicles of various makes — Leyland,

AEC, Commer, Dennis, FWD, etc, in addition to the driving of steam wagons. However, during the summer months I did a considerable amount of charabanc work on both private hire and excursions, a job which I enjoyed immensely. In those far-off days it was quite customary for drivers to do their own running repairs, and indeed, to carry out overhauls – making many mistakes of course, but learning from them. After reaching the age of 21 my job became still more varied, embracing the canvassing and tendering for the removal side of the business and also doing a fair amount of funeral work – my uncles acquired a taxi and funeral business in 1918. Then came the big change in my life.

Buses in Harrogate It was towards the end of May, 1922 that my uncles told me that I was required to go to Harrogate to run a bus business. Two Leyland RAF type chassis with Leyland 'Edinburgh' type bodies were on order and two charabancs were to be transferred from Halifax for excursion and private hire work. I was informed that a supplier of spare parts (Mr Firth Crossley) who resided in Harrogate, had persuaded them to start this new business and had obtained licences to operate a circular service between Harrogate and Bilton. Apparently, the original idea was that Mr Crossley would manage the business, but he subsequently decided to be only nominally manager but responsible for the book-keeping side of the business.

I went to Harrogate at the end of May, by which time one charabanc had been transferred and a driver engaged for private hire and excursion work. A small garage had been leased in Mornington Crescent. As delivery of the two buses was expected within a fortnight I had to obtain the necessary staff as quickly as possible. I engaged two drivers, three conductors and one cleaner. The service was of a 10-minutes frequency from 7.35 am to 8.5 pm, then every 30 minutes until 10.5 pm. I calculated that if I relieved the two drivers for an hour each at lunch time, relieved one for tea and then took over from the other driver and worked through to finish, the job could be done with a minimum of staff. No service was operated on Sundays as no local services were permitted by Harrogate Corporation on that day. The cashing in of conductors was carried out by Mr Crossley or a member of his staff. After three months there was a severe fire and the garage and four vehicles were burned out, being subsequently replaced in about two months' time, hired vehicles covering the operation in the interim period. Soon after this, Mr Crossley packed up altogether, so I became manager, taking on the clerical duties but passing on some of the driving to the cleaner whom I had trained. It is appropriate to mention here that a network of services in the Harrogate area was at that time operated by the Harrogate Road Car Co Ltd, their chief services being to Knaresborough, Starbeck, Oatlands, Mount, Harlow Hill, Duchy Road, New Park and Bilton, the last being started up after we had obtained licences.

In April, 1924, Tillings purchased a controlling interest in the Harrogate Road Car Co Ltd and in the Harrogate Carriage Company, and also purchased our business, much to my disappointment. I was promised a job by Mr Walter Wolsey if I wished to stay on, but preferred to stay for one month only, until the route was absorbed by the Harrogate Road Car Company.

The Start of Hebble I returned to Halifax in May, 1924, when I informed my uncles that I did not wish to carry on permanently with haulage but would much prefer that they launched out in the bus business locally. They said they were quite prepared to do this if I could suggest suitable routes.

It will be appreciated that in 1924 Halifax Corporation had around 100 trams covering a fairly wide area and linked up with Bradford Corporation at Shelf, at Queensbury and at Bailiff Bridge, and with Huddersfield Corporation at West Vale and at Brighouse. Halifax operated buses to Siddal and also to Wainstalls from Pellon. Further, Yorkshire (Woollen District) Electric Tramways Ltd were expanding rapidly, but not having been able to obtain licences to run into Halifax their buses were poised on the doorstep at Hipperholme, only 2½ miles away. However, I eventually recommended that we should apply for licences to run from Halifax to Brighouse via Southowram, this being the most direct but most hilly route between the two towns and only served by Halifax Corporation tramways for a distance of 1½ miles to Southowram (Bank Top). Halifax Corporation had, however, a through tram service to Brighouse via Hipperholme. I also recommended the operation of a route from Halifax to Bingley via Holmfield, Bradshaw, Denholme, Cullingworth and Harden. Licences were quickly obtained from all the outside authorities, but refused by Halifax County Borough. Nevertheless, orders were placed for four 38-seater and two 26-seater Leylands and a plot of land purchased in Commercial Street (main street) for use as a terminal stand. The operation of these two services was commenced by Hebble Bus Services on 1 December 1924, and although no licences were held in Halifax, passengers were picked up in the county borough. However, so far as the Brighouse route was concerned, no passengers were picked up in the borough except those who, on the outward journey, booked for points outside the borough (which only extended some 1½ miles). On the Bingley route, the county borough extended 4½ miles, but the bus route left the tram route a mile and a half from the town centre, so passengers were picked up on the outward journey for setting down after leaving the tram track, and on the inward journey until the tram track was reached. From the very beginning, the two routes were well patronised, particularly between Southowram Village and Halifax on the Brighouse route and between Bradshaw, Holmfield and Halifax on the Bingley route. After about a fortnight's operation the police pounced. They first brought cases before the court for plying for hire in the county borough on the Bingley route where passengers were being picked up and set down within the borough, but of course not on the tram track. Fines were imposed, so it was decided to change the route of the Bingley service so as to proceed direct along the tram track, which was the shortest route, there being no point in deviating via Bradshaw and Holmfield when passengers could not be picked up. The method then adopted was as for the Brighouse route, namely, that the passengers picked up in the borough were those who, on the outward journey, wished to travel beyond the borough boundary. As a result of the alteration of route the revenue on the Bingley service decreased considerably. Next the police took action in respect of passengers picked up in the borough for travel to points outside, and again fines were imposed. It was then decided that only persons who had obtained tickets in advance at the booking office on the private land would be picked up in the county borough. After this method had been in operation a few weeks, the police took action once again and heavy fines were imposed. The publicity resulting from all these police actions was actually beneficial to the company and patronage increased, but some way had to be found to keep the services going in and out of Halifax.

It was therefore decided that the only passengers picked up in the borough would be those holding return tickets booked from outside areas in which licences were held. It took some time for passengers to get used to the system and many had to be politely refused permission to board the buses when not holding return tickets. The revenue on the Brighouse route did not suffer at all by the change of system as the borough only extended about 1½ miles, but the Bingley route suffered very badly indeed. Whilst all this business of prosecution was in progress, applications had been made to run from Halifax to Greetland and Halifax to Elland. Licences were quickly obtained from all the local authorities, with the exception of Halifax, and these two new routes were opened in the spring of 1925 and operated on the return ticket system. Two more Leyland 26-seaters were purchased and the fleet augmented by a Daimler 20-seater and a Leyland 28-seater chara, previously used for private hire.

The Elland and Greetland routes were immediately successful and were soon extended to Huddersfield and to Barkisland respectively, but without licences in the County Borough of Huddersfield. We therefore had the odd position of a half-hourly service between the two important towns of Halifax and Huddersfield while only holding licences issued by Elland UDC, situated between them.

However, as the services were such a boon to the public, they quickly found out that if they were regular travellers they had only to make their way once by tramcar to West Vale, change there for Elland, then travel by bus and take a return ticket from there to Huddersfield, then on the return journey book return from Elland to Halifax and use the return half the following day, after which there was no difficulty whatever.

Nevertheless, the method of operation was not really satisfactory and appeals were lodged with the Ministry of Transport against the refusal of licences by the County Borough of Halifax in respect of the routes to Brighouse, to Bingley, to Barkisland and to Elland/Huddersfield, and against Huddersfield Corporation for refusal of licences for the Huddersfield/Halifax service. Subsequently the Minister appointed Mr R.H. Tolerton to hold an inquiry in Halifax, as a result of which Halifax issued licences for these routes but with protective fares for the tramway undertakings. Following the decision of the Minister the Halifax/Elland/Huddersfield route became jointly operated as follows:

50 per cent - Hebble
25 per cent - Halifax Corporation
25 per cent - Huddersfield Corporation.

The joint service between Halifax and Huddersfield commenced in October, 1925.

After the granting of these licences, the terminal points of the services concerned were changed to Alexandra Street and King Edward Street. Almost immediately after the issue of licences on these routes, applications were submitted for the operation of new services from Halifax to Luddenden and from Halifax to Beech Road, Sowerby Bridge. Once again the urban authorities quickly granted the necessary licences, but Halifax refused and the services were inaugurated on the return ticket system. The routes operated by Hebble at the end of 1925 were, therefore as follows:

Halifax/Elland/Huddersfield (Jointly with Halifax and Huddersfield Corporations)	Fully licensed
Halifax/Southowram/Brighouse	Fully licensed
Halifax/Denholme/Bingley	Fully licensed
Halifax/Greetland/Barkisland	Fully licensed
Halifax/Luddenden/Midgley	Return ticket system
Halifax/Beech Road, Sowerby Bridge	Return ticket system

The fleet strength of eight Leyland single-deckers, plus a number of unsuitable charabancs, was inadequate for the proper coverage of these routes, so an order was placed for a number of Albion 'Vikings' of the bonneted type, these vehicles being specially designed for passenger work, with lighter chassis and pneumatic tyres and a 30/60 hp engine with detachable cylinder heads. I rather think that the Albion 'Viking' was produced in advance of the Leyland PLSC.1. The delivery of these vehicles commenced in the spring of 1926. Then came a stroke of luck so far as Hebble was concerned, namely, the effect of the General Strike of 1926. At that time Hebble had no agreement with any Trades Union, and no Union had ever made an approach. Consequently, although the Corporation Passenger Transport Undertakings came to a standstill, and also the British Electric Traction companies, Hebble kept going and reaped a rare harvest. Routes were immediately opened to Bradford via Shelf, Leeds via Dudley Hill, and Manchester via Todmorden and Rochdale. Young businessmen volunteered and were taken on as temporary bus drivers. Some were first-class, some were 'anything but'. I had the most hectic three weeks of my life and worked myself to the bone. However, the result of all this was that after the strike was over, we continued our services to Bradford and to Leeds but were quickly hoofed out of Manchester.

We were soon granted licences in Bradford (with protection for tramways) but Halifax did not grant licences for a considerable time; however as ample protection was given to the tram services, the corporation did not take any action against us or try to stop our operation.

We were permitted to keep going in Leeds whilst an application was passing through the normal channels, but we were eventually refused by the council, even though it was understood that the appropriate committee had given the application its blessing. However, the service was licensed in Halifax, in the Bradford area and in Pudsey UD, so it was kept going into Leeds on the return ticket system. Halifax also granted licences for Yorkshire (Woollen District) to run to Leeds via Cleckheaton, so we had competition with a BET company for the first time for terminal traffic.

By this time the fleet had increased by the purchase of a number of Albion 32-seater buses with side type controls. Bodies were of various makes — Massey Bros, Fielding & Bottomley, Snapes and Barnaby. The nett price of a chassis in those days was around £650 and as my uncles would never pay more than £1,000 for a complete vehicle, the body makers had of course to tender for no more than £350 or they would not get the order. Anyhow, we got what we paid for and no more. Meanwhile, vehicle accommodation was becoming a real problem and so was maintenance. No additional premises had been acquired since the Hebble Bus Services had started, although the fleet had then reached around thirty vehicles. Maintenance of chassis had to be carried out under very poor conditions at the haulage depot in South Darley Street, whilst washing and body repairs were carried out at the funeral department at Gibbet Hill, where there was also covered accommodation for not more than three buses in addition to the considerable number of taxis, hire cars and motor hearses. The balance of vehicles had to be parked in the open at the ground in Commercial Street.

Expansion Meanwhile we were looking around for fresh fields to conquer, and during the latter part in 1926 opened up a new fully licensed route for a change, between Queensbury, Thornton, Allerton and Bingley, operation being at two-hourly frequencies. The revenue on the route was far below the standard of other services, and many alterations were carried out in succeeding years.

In January, 1927, we started a half-hourly service between Brighouse and Bradford, being fully licensed but giving ample protection to the Bradford Corporation Tramways undertaking between Bradford and Bailiff Bridge. However, the success of the Hebble return ticket system of operation on certain routes into Halifax had been noticed by other operators and prospective operators, as a result of which, Messrs John Hirst (Ripponden & District) and Ryburn Haulage and Garage Co Ltd, both operating between Ripponden and Sowerby Bridge, extended their services into Halifax on the return ticket system. Neither was competitive with the Hebble routes, but an entirely new operator started towards the end of 1926, namely the Calder Bus Company, who, for a period of about two years, caused a real headache to many undertakings. Calder introduced services from Brighouse to Bradford via Bailiff Bridge, to Huddersfield and to Bradford via Hipperholme and Shelf, all on the return ticket system, and also between Wyke, Hipperholme and Halifax. The two routes between Brighouse and Bradford were both competitive with Hebble.

Early in 1927 an hourly service was introduced between Halifax and Heptonstall, a village perched on a hilltop and overlooking Hebden Bridge. The route followed the Halifax Corporation tram service for the whole of the seven miles between Halifax and Hebden Bridge and was, of course, operated on the return ticket system, and a winner right from the start. We quickly followed up with an hourly service at the opposite half-hour between Halifax, Hebden Bridge and Blackshaw Head, the latter being some two miles beyond Heptonstall over the moors in the direction of Burnley;

A Garage at Last At long last my uncles realised that something had to be done to provide covered accommodation for the vehicles, especially as there was grave risk of vehicle maintenance falling down completely. Consequently, a large old building covering an area of 42,000 sq ft and with a yard of 11,000 sq ft, was purchased in Walnut Street, Halifax, this being about one mile from the centre of the town. The premises had previously been used as a dye-works by a subsidiary of the Bradford Dyers Association. The building was really in two halves, divided by a two-storey structure in the centre. The roof of each building was supported by rows of pillars about 15 ft apart, and it was eventually decided to completely scrap the roof over one half and fit an entirely new one and at the same time lay a concrete floor and carry out other constructional alterations.

The building was first used as a bus garage in August, 1927, by which time the fleet was of such a size that the modified half of the building was full up from the beginning, but nevertheless the improvement in ease of operation can only be fully realised by persons who know what it is like to operate and maintain a fleet of buses virtually without any accommodation or maintenance facilities.

In the early summer of 1927 it was decided to apply for an extension of the Halifax/Blackshaw route through to Burnley — an added distance of nine miles. Between Blackshaw Head and Mereclough (six miles) the road is over the Pennines, rising to an altitude of around 1,400 ft. There are no villages whatever over the six miles stretch, and only scattered farms. Burnley Corporation had a bus service extending a distance of 2½ miles towards Mereclough. It was decided to offer generous protection to the Burnley Corporation undertaking and thus there was no difficulty in obtaining licences. The route was opened in August, 1927 — not without mixed feelings as to its financial possibilities. The frequency was every hour during the summer months and every two hours in winter, alternate buses turning round at Blackshaw Head so as to provide an hourly frequency between there and Halifax all the year round. The patronage over the sparsely populated section exceeded expectations, as also the volume of through traffic between Halifax, Hebden Bridge and Burnley. By 1931 the hourly service was maintained throughout the year.

From the very commencement of the operation of the Halifax/Bingley service in 1924 there were other operators between Harden and Bingley and also between Wilsden, Harden and Bingley. Actually, there were far more operators than the traffic could stand, and after about two years the Wilsden/Bingley operation was confined to two branches of a family called Brigg. One branch obtained licences to extend from Wilsden to the centre of Bradford in 1926 and the other to extend from Wilsden to Duckworth Lane tram terminus, being about two miles from the centre of the city. Subsequently, Hugh Brigg purchased the business of his relative, after which the firm was known as Hugh Brigg & Sons. In 1928 we learnt that they were prepared to sell out, so negotiations were inaugurated and the business purchased, the take-over being made on 26 May 1928. The fleet operated by Brigg consisted of a number of Leyland Lions, a Dennis 'E' type and a Gotfredson. As the running of these two new services could not economically be operated from Halifax, it was arranged that the vehicles be garaged at Messrs J.W. North Ltd, Legrams Lane, Bradford – a firm in which O. & C. Holdsworth had a large financial interest.

The route Halifax/Bradford via Shelf, started in May, 1926, had proved most successful, in spite of most generous protection being given to the two tramway undertakings. There was a large amount of through traffic between the two towns, so early in 1928 applications were made for a new service to Bradford via Queensbury. The applications were successful and the new route opened in July, 1928. The service quickly proved to be even better than the old route via Shelf. The combined frequencies between Halifax and Bradford were every 15 minutes in the morning and every 10 minutes thereafter.

During 1928 Bradford Corporation acquired the business of the Calder bus undertaking, but came up against the difficulty of obtaining licences in Halifax and Huddersfield, where Calder had also been refused. Bradford therefore entered into an arrangement for Hebble to operate the Halifax/Wyke route and also the Brighouse, Hipperholme/Bradford route as between Hipperholme and Bradford, on their behalf at a fixed rate per mile. Eventually, Hebble agreed to purchase these two routes from Bradford Corporation, together with all the ex-Calder rolling stock, the sale being effective from 1 October 1928.

Meanwhile, an appeal had been lodged by Hebble with the Ministry of Transport against the refusal of Huddersfield Corporation to grant a licence to operate between Bradford, Brighouse and Huddersfield, being in effect an extension of an existing service.

An inquiry was held by the Ministry of Transport on 20 October 1927, following which a 15-minute service was commenced on 6 December 1927, between Bradford, Brighouse and Huddersfield, the operation being equally shared between Bradford Corporation, Huddersfield Corporation and Hebble.

It is interesting to record that no pooling arrangement was made at the time, and as far as I know, no such arrangement has been introduced since. Each operator looked after the duplication of his own timings, when necessary.

Prior to the start of Hebble in 1924, O. & C. Holdsworth had operated what we now term 'period excursions' to Blackpool, chiefly during the local 'Wakes' or holiday weeks. Actually, the operation started during the first World War with steam wagons on which charabanc bodies were merely dropped on to the fixed flat lorries. This operation was continued and the period of operation gradually extended. In May, 1928, a daily service was introduced between Halifax, Hebden Bridge and Blackpool, starting at 8 am from Halifax and returning from Blackpool at 6 pm, which enabled day excursionists to be carried in addition to period passengers. The service was quite successful and by 1929 was operated all the year round.

With the steady increase in the size of the Hebble fleet, further constructional improvements were carried out at the Walnut Street depot and a new roof fitted over the major portion of the remaining half of the premises, providing covered accommodation for a total of sixty buses.

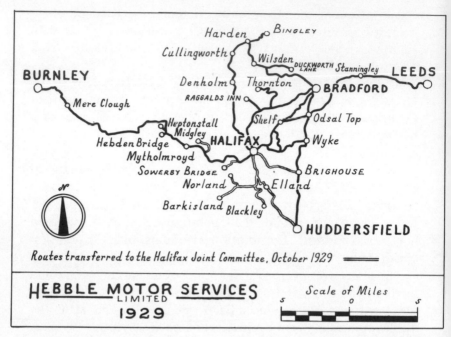

(Fig 2) Map of Hebble services, 1929. Drawn by E. Axten after data in published time tables

By the middle of 1928 Hebble were operating on twenty routes and I felt the future was really bright, with greatly improved organisation which had been built up from scratch over a period of some 3½ years. I was soon to be disullusioned.

The Railways Appear The Railways obtained general powers to run bus services in August, 1928, to enable them to combat the ever-increasing competition throughout the country. This included powers to enter into arrangements with existing operators. They soon turned their attention to the West Riding of Yorkshire. During that year they sounded the Halifax Corporation, who, apparently, were interested in making some arrangements. Negotiations were started which were protracted, but apparently broad principles were fairly quickly agreed. Whilst these negotiations were still in progress, the Railways approached O. & C. Holdsworth who, with 'horse deal' blood in their veins, were by no means averse to

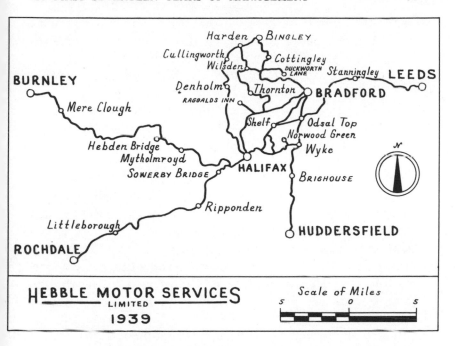

(Fig 3) Map of Hebble services, 1939. Drawn by E. Axten after data in published time tables

'overture for purchase,' being well able to negotiate favourable terms for an eventual transaction. The railway negotiations with Halifax Corporation and with Holdsworths, ran broadly parallel, but those with Holdsworths were the first to be completed, namely, on 30 April 1929, but the actual take-over date reverted to 1 January 1929. The railways took over seventytwo buses, two charabancs and the garage in Walnut Street. The agreement with Halifax Corporation was made on 11 May 1929, and its terms affected the Hebble operation materially.

It is not for me to go into any detail relating to the agreement with the Halifax Corporation, but the salient features were as follows:

(1) All bus services starting and finishing within the Halifax County Borough to be operated solely by Halifax Corporation, such to be known as 'A' services.

(2) All services starting within the County Borough of Halifax and extending to the boundary of an area known as 'B' to be jointly and equally operated by Halifax Corporation and the railways, such services being controlled by a Joint Committee

(3) All services from the County Borough of Halifax and extending outside the 'B' area, to be operated by the railways or their nominees, and to be known as 'C' services.

There was, however, one exception, namely, the Halifax/Elland/Huddersfield route, of which Hebble had operated 50 per cent since 1925. Although, according to the defined area, this service fell within the category of 'C', the agreement provided for its transfer from Hebble to the Halifax Joint Committee. As a result of the terms of this agreement, the following Hebble routes were transferred to the Halifax Joint Committee on 6 November 1929, together with a number of vehicles:

Halifax/Barkisland and Norland via Greetland
Halifax/Brighouse via Southowram
Halifax/Huddersfield via Elland
Halifax/Midgley via Luddenfoot
Halifax/Beech Road (Sowerby Bridge)
Halifax/Hullen Edge and Blackley via West Vale
Halifax/Heptonstall

After these routes were transferred to the Joint Committee, my uncles informed me that I could return with them to the haulage business if I so desired. I told them that my heart was in the bus business and not in haulage and that under the circumstances I would stay on with Hebble. I shall never know whether my decision in 1929 was right or not, but from the standpoint of happiness, I have had no regrets.

Thus ended my fifteen years' experience with my uncles who, up to that time, had cared little about statistics but had the knack of guiding businesses in a successful direction.

It was not until 1 January 1930 that the railways took control of Hebble, as it was arranged that O. & C. Holdsworth should supervise the business until the end of 1929. The change was very marked indeed. The railway accountants made their presence felt but did not seem to appreciate the serious effect on the profitability of the company caused by the loss of seven routes out of a total of twenty. Further, the vehicle maintenance and overhaul programme had to follow the pattern and procedure used by the railways in respect of their fleet of goods vehicles, most of which only covered short hauls. The revenue per mile went down and the operating costs per mile went up and there was little I could do to alter things. However, there was one relatively small but important happening which was to be to the eventual benefit of Hebble. We took over three Leyland Tiger coaches which had been ordered by the railways for their own use; two had bodies by Eastern Counties and one by Hall Lewis. At that time I considered these coaches to be the best I had ever seen, and far better than any in the surrounding district. They gave a tremendous boost to our private hire business, which, from that time started to grow and never looked back.

After the railway acquisition of Hebble, it became necessary to find alternative accommodation in Bradford as the arrangements made with Messrs J.W. North Ltd could not continue.

We eventually leased a garage from the West Yorkshire Road Car Co in Edderthorpe Street, which had been acquired by them in the purchase of Blythe & Berwick Ltd, but vacated following the construction of an entirely new garage. The garage was of adequate size for our requirements, with accommodation for sixteen vehicles. It had the disadvantage of being on a very severe slope but had access from streets at each end, which would not have been possible if the site had been levelled.

I once gave the railways a real fright. It was, I believe, in 1930 when the normal day excursion fare charged by road to Blackpool was 7s. Price cutting started by our competitors, first to 6s, then to 5s, then to 4s. I considered it time that something was done to put a stop to this so I advertised a Sunday excursion to Blackpool at the fare of 2s 6d and booked hundreds of passengers within hours. The railways got to know about this and the telephone was red hot with calls from the railways at Manchester and at London, instructing me to withdraw the excursion, being told that it was they (the railways) who were the people to run excursions at low rates. I told them that as the passengers were booked I could not cancel them. However, I received instructions that nothing of the sort should occur again. As it turned out, the instructions were unnecessary as the slashing of the fare for one day put an end to rate cutting by our competitors.

BET Take Over The railways, having made satisfactory arrangements for financial holdings in many BET and Tilling Bus Companies, no longer desired to be the sole owners and controllers of the Hebble Company. As a result, the private company of Hebble Motor Services Ltd was registered on 19 July 1930, but the agreement for the take-over of the railway-owned Hebble Company was not made until 22 February 1932, from which date, although the railways retained 50 per cent financial interest in the business, the control went over to the BET.

I still have vivid recollections of one incident which occurred at the Board meeting on 22 February 1932. Everything obviously had been cut and dried before the meeting, and for the most part the proceedings were quite formal. Only one question was asked and this followed the taking over of the senior members of the staff, including myself. The question put by a BET Director (now deceased) was: 'What notice are these staff on?' which brought forth the reply from the Chairman (Mr P.M. Rossdale): 'One month, Sir.'

I left the meeting with the feeling that my days as manager of Hebble Motor Services Ltd were numbered.

About a month later, Mr John Spencer Wills, a director of the company, spent several days with me. Quite honestly, he scared me stiff. It was soon obvious to me that Mr Wills knew a great deal about the bus business and it was just as quickly obvious that the main object of his visit was to find out just how much I knew about the business. Since 1929 the company had not done at all well, and it was soon apparent that such a state of affairs would not be allowed to continue. I was instructed to prepare a report, showing estimated results for the following three years, indicating where and how revenue could be improved and where and how expenditure could be reduced. I duly completed the report and sent it to Mr Wills. Sufficient is to say that from that time the company quickly pulled round and my estimates were not only fulfilled , but exceeded.

Thus started my long and happy connection with BET, which led to my becoming the longest-serving general manager in the BET Group of Companies.

During the summer of 1929 (this being in the early period of railway ownership) a daily express service had been introduced — between Halifax and Scarborough. Calls were made at the railway stations in Leeds and York and the terminal point in Scarborough was at the railway station. However, according to records, the service was discontinued after one season's operation. My mind is not clear as to why the service was suspended, but I rather think it was at the request of the railways, who in the latter part of 1929 were in negotiation with the BET and Tilling Companies.

The Scarborough service catered for passengers between Leeds and Scarborough and between York and Scarborough and I imagine would not be looked upon with favour by West Yorkshire. However, after the passing of the Road Traffic Act in 1930, Hebble applied for a Todmorden/Halifax/Scarborough service, but this was withdrawn upon instructions from the railways. However, I agreed with Yorkshire WD for them to apply for the service, with the last picking up point at Stanningley. The application was granted but the service was operated by Hebble 'On Hire to Yorkshire WD.' After Hebble became BET controlled an application was then submitted to the Traffic Commissioners for a licence to operate the Scarborough service previously licensed to Yorkshire WD, the application being granted on 9 December 1932.

On 3 December 1928, the LM&S Railway took over the bus service between Halifax and Rochdale via Ripponden and Blackstone Edge, previously operated by Halifax Corporation from August 1926 to February 1928 and afterwards by Rochdale Corporation to December 1928. Both corporations had had to surrender the service because of inability to obtain licences in Soyland. The LM&S operated the service at irregular frequencies and used the railway stations at Rochdale and at Halifax as terminal points.

During 1933 the LM&S Railway approached Hebble to see whether an arrangement could be made for the route to be transferred. The revenue at that time was around 5d per mile and therefore the route was by no means attractive. However, in view of the success of the Halifax/Burnley service, I considered that the route had possibilities so eventually take-over terms were agreed and Hebble operation commenced on 10 December 1933.

It had been agreed with the railways that the station terminals would be discontinued, and also that the service would be operated at a regular hourly frequency. The length of the route was sixteen miles and the timetable provided for the outward journey to be covered in 56 minutes with four minutes lay-over in Rochdale, and the inward journey in 58 minutes, with two minutes lay-over in Halifax. I knew before the route was started that with existing rolling stock buses would run a few minutes late on busy trips and that a spare bus would have to be ready to take up the running from Halifax on such occasions. However, I was convinced that this was a minor drawback compared with the advantages of operating at a regular frequency. Within three months it was apparent that the route was going to be a winner and shortly after we acquired a number of Albion single-deckers with much larger engines and the initial operating difficulties were quickly overcome. There was, however, one snag which arose, namely, that the new type Albions were so much faster than the former type that on quiet trips, drivers ran ahead of time over the moors. The problem was solved by the installation of a time clock at the top of Blackstone Edge and drivers had to use clock cards. Traffic on the route on fine week-ends quickly got so heavy that we operated the route with lowbridge double-deckers at these busy times. There is an arched bridge on the approach to Littleborough but this caused no difficulty as there was sufficient clearance, provided the drivers did not hug the side of the road. However, after operating about three months, the North Western Traffic Commissioners advised us that they were to survey the route as specific permission had to be obtained to operate double-deckers in their area. There was a joint inspection of the route but permission was refused because of the arched bridge.

In August, 1933 the traffic commissioners granted applications for both the Rochdale/Halifax and Burnley/Halifax routes to be linked up with the half-hourly service between Halifax and Leeds, thus providing for an hourly through service between Rochdale/Halifax and Leeds and an hourly through service between Burnley/Halifax and Leeds. All three routes concerned benefited by the changes.

It is interesting to recall that in November 1932 Hebble made an application for an increase of certain fares, prompted by an increase of 3d per gallon in the price of petrol. No solicitor was engaged and I took the application in January 1933 with a certain amount of trepidation. The chairman (Mr Joseph Farndale) looked anything but pleased but nevertheless granted the application at the hearing. However, he announced that he did not welcome applications for increases of fares and as far as I know, no other operators in the area ever applied for increases until after the War. It was not very long before petrol reverted to its former price, so applications were made, and granted, for fares to be reduced to their former level.

In the early 'thirties, there was a tremendous amount of competition between express operators from the chief Yorkshire towns to Blackpool. West Yorkshire had joint services with Ribble, via Keighley and Burnley, Yorkshire Traction, Yorkshire WD, and Hebble operated independently via Todmorden and Burnley, and in addition there were the services of Wallace Arnold, Hansons, Bullock & Sons, Pyne's and many others, the latter mostly week-end operators. In addition, Armitage, Walker Taylor and Wood Bros operated to Yorkshire from the Blackpool end. Eventually it became known that the operators in Blackpool were not averse to 'doing a deal' and their businesses were acquired and absorbed in a Pool comprising Ribble, West Yorkshire, Yorkshire Traction, Yorkshire WD and Hebble Companies. Timetables were redrafted and co-ordinated and although the scheme was turned down by the traffic commissioners it was successful on appeal. Pool operation commenced on 1 December 1934.

By 1934 the two Halifax/Bradford routes, with a combined ten minutes frequency and operated with double-deckers, had become so popular that much Saturday duplication had to be provided. A Saturday only service at half-hourly frequencies via Shelf and Wibsey was therefore introduced in August of that year, the route being half a mile shorter than the other two routes, which enabled the return journey to be covered in one hour. The route became extremely popular for through passengers and was known as the 'Wibsey Flyer' although its timetabled speed was no more than 16 mph.

The Bradford via Wibsey route was the last new stage carriage service to be introduced up to the time that I left the company at the end of May 1939. It will be appreciated that the expansion of the Hebble company was not only affected by the agreement between the railways and Halifax Corporation, but also because the company was surrounded by other companies in either BET, BAT or Tilling Groups, namely Yorkshire Woollen District, West Yorkshire, North Western and Ribble. Nevertheless the period was one of consolidation and growth of existing services as 'passengers carried' increased by over 50 per cent between 1933 and 1939 and mileage by 24 per cent. The recreational side of the business showed a considerable expansion as mileage on contract and excursion work increased by 80 per cent and with a fleet of fourteen coaches we had become the largest private hire and excursion operator in the Halifax area. The excursion business had been strengthened by the acquisition of R. Edwards & Co Ltd in October 1934, this company being controlled by Wrights of Burnley.

Whilst the loss of seven routes to the Halifax Joint Committee in 1929 was a severe blow to the company, it had the effect of necessitating the development of the business on express, contract and excursion work, with the result that when I left the company in 1939 it was in a most healthy state, with a fleet strength of seventy vehicles, almost identical with that of 1929.

Although Hebble remained a relatively small company, its varied type of operation made it an ideal company for the gaining of experience by young general managers. The following succeeded me in the order shown:

	Subsequent position
Mr C.R.H. Wreathall	General Manager of East Yorks Motor Services Ltd
Mr A.J. White	General Manager of Maidstone & District Motor Services Ltd
Mr I.L. Gray	General Manager of Rhondda Transport Co Ltd
Mr F.K. Pointon	General Manager of East Midland Motor Services Ltd

It was also interesting to recall that Mr W.M. Dravers, later a director of many BET companies, was traffic manager at Hebble from 1935 to 1939. He afterwards became general manager of Sheffield United Tours, South Wales Transport Company and Maidstone & District, before reaching his subsequent elevated position at Stratton House.

PASSENGER TRANSPORT IN BRISTOL IN THE VICTORIAN ERA

T. W. H. Gailey

This paper was read to the Omnibus Society in 1956, when Mr Gailey, now Chief Executive of the National Bus Company, was Traffic Manager of the Bristol Tramways and Carriage Company. The quality of public transport in a Victorian city is made clear in this study of a remarkable undertaking that — as the Bristol Omnibus Company — remains active at the present day.

A few years ago I was browsing around a secondhand book-shop in Bristol and found two interesting books on the early history of the City. The first was a book published in 1794 entitled *Mathews' 'New History of Bristol'* which contained a fascinating account of the City at the end of the eighteenth century, and the other was a handbook prepared by the Bristol Tramways & Carriage Co (as it then was) in 1897 to commemorate the Diamond Jubilee of Queen Victoria. These two publications gave me an insight into the life of Bristol during the nineteenth century and set me off researching into how people got around in those days. I was thus able to form some judgment of the revolutionary changes which occurred in public transport during that period and to convince myself that operational problems were nothing new.

At the end of the eighteenth century, Bristol with an estimated population of 100,000 was a city of some importance and of considerable prosperity. It ranked in size next to London. The computed population of other cities at that time was: Birmingham 60,000; Liverpool 47,000; Norwich 38,000; Bath 25,000; Leeds 18,000. Nevertheless, the main part of the city covered a relatively small area and in those more austere days the need for internal transport was not recognised. The richer citizens rode on horse back and the rest walked. As William Mathews expressed it in 1794, there were ample 'conveniences for ambulatory exercitation.' Only in 1786 did the first hackney carriages begin to stand in the streets, and by the end of the century their number had reached 30, dispersed in 12 stands in various parts of the city. Passenger transport to other towns and cities was of course provided by stage coaches, variously known as post coaches and mail coaches, whilst the carriage of goods and merchandise depended upon a varied and comprehensive service of 'waggons' through the length and breadth of the country. Mathews records a very elaborate programme of regular passenger stage coach services from Bristol to such destinations as London, Birmingham, Oxford, Exeter, Portsmouth, Weymouth, Bath, Wells and Gloucester, and these naturally served a large number of other towns intermediately on their routes. There were, for instance, sixteen departures daily for Bath and six departures daily for London, including one coach which by leaving at 4 am apparently managed to complete the journey in one day. Incidentally, it is worth noting that 4 am was not considered an unreasonably early departure time in those days as coaches were scheduled to leave at that time for Birmingham, Portsmouth and Bath, as well as for London.

In a guide to Bristol published by the Reverend John Evans in 1814, it is interesting to read that the number of stage coaches had increased and additional towns were being served. The 'one day' coach to London seems, however, to have disappeared — probably because of its inability to maintain its ambitious schedule on the very indifferent roads. The progress and development of these stage coach services during those twenty years from 1794 are reflected in the increasing dignity of the announcements. The stage coaches which previously left from the Bush Tavern, Corn Street, now are recorded as departing from the Bush Tavern Coach Office. A number of the coaches are given names such as 'Loyal

Volunteer' to London, 'The Cambrian' to Swansea, 'The Duke of York Coach' to Exeter, and 'The Royal Devonshire Coach' — forerunners no doubt of the later custom of named trains on the railways. There was of course no lack of competition in those days and it is not surprising to find references to 'Fromonts' London Opposition Coach' and to 'Fromonts' Cheap Bath Coach'. In addition to the scheduled services of stage coaches, most of the proprietors were prepared 'to accommodate families at their own hours', ie to run 'private hire' coaches. I even found a reference to excursions and tours in the eighteenth century when Mathews in 1794 mentioned that 'the various stage and hackney coaches will accommodate those persons or parties who are for a pleasant ride into the country.'

The birth of the first urban passenger transport system in Bristol was not easy. Although in London horse buses had commenced to run in the year 1829, it was not until 1871 that the first proposals for street transport in Bristol were considered by the Corporation. These proposals came from two large firms who were referred to by the local newspapers somewhat impolitely as 'London Speculators.' They applied for powers to construct tramways on a very extensive scale in Bristol, but the City Council considered that the services could well be provided by local people and both the schemes were rejected. The corporation and Messrs Stanley & Wasbrough then obtained powers for the construction of tramways in the city. The corporation's powers were to borrow £14,000 to construct a tramway from Old Market Street along West Street and Lawrence Hill to the city boundary and also a tramway from St Augustine's Place along Colston Street, Perry Road, Park Row and Whiteladies Road to St John's Church, Redland. Soon after their bill was passed however there was a considerable advance in the price of iron and other material and the corporation could only finance one line with the money authorised. They decided to construct the Redland line which was completed by the spring of 1874 and to let the powers for the Old Market Street line lapse. The powers obtained by Messrs Stanley & Wasbrough were to construct a tramway from Fishponds to Kingswood, linking up with the line proposed by the corporation from Old Market Street. As the corporation were not proceeding with this second line, Messrs Stanley & Wasbrough had to withdraw their proposals as well, since they had no power to get into Bristol other than by the line proposed by the corporation. Such were some of the obstacles which the pioneers came up against in seeking to provide urban transport in Bristol.

The troubles were by no means over however. For various reasons the corporation were unwilling to operate the tramways service themselves and they now had to find someone to do so.* Various prominent citizens were approached, but they were reluctant to pay the price which the corporation demanded to reimburse them for the heavy capital expenditure on the line, but eventually in July, 1874, a few responsible persons agreed to form a company for the purpose. In return they required certain concessions from the corporation, amongst them being a claim for the use of the tramway free of charge for seven years. No better offer was forthcoming and at first the council refused to entertain this proposition. The promoters of the intended company thereupon abated their demands and in October an arrangement was entered into by which the council granted the company a lease of the tramway for twentyone years, the first five years being free of charge, and the rent for the remainder of the term rising at intervals from £360 to a maximum of £600 a year.

At the same time the council sanctioned the construction by the company of a tramway from Old Market Street to St George, with a branch to Eastville, and another line from Castle Street to Perry Road to link up with the Redland line. These schemes to the astonishment of the company, were

---

* The main reason why the corporation did not wish to operate was financial. The council was divided on the matter and could not obtain adequate borrowing powers to meet the heavy expenditure involved (including the cost of a Private Bill).

opposed in Parliament by certain shopkeepers who, being anxious about the possible effects on their trade, contended that it would be a great inconvenience to them that a tramway should pass along Lawrence Hill. Other opponents of the Bill in Parliament were advocates of 'Sabbath' observance who strongly objected to Sunday travelling, whilst a few persons quite openly opposed the scheme from a dread of the influx into the fashionable suburbs of working men and their families on holidays. Both the company and the corporation thought that these objections were unreasonable and pursued their proposals vigorously. A Board of Trade Inquiry was held and the Bristol Council petitioned Parliament in support of the Bill with the result that eventually the tramways were approved.

And so the first tramway operating between Perry Road and Redland was triumphantly opened on the 9 August 1875. And it was no mean triumph for the newly created Bristol Tramways Company. All along the route flags had been hoisted, many of which bore such appropriate inscriptions as 'Success to the Tramways'. At 12 o'clock the Mayor and other members of the corporation as well as other prominent citizens travelled in the first cars. Each car was drawn by four splendid horses in new harness and the uniform of the drivers and conductors was of a greyish colour with scarlet trimmings.

The company commenced operations with a fleet of six tramcars, although only three had been delivered on the opening day. The trams were built by the Starbuck Car Company of Leamington. Each of the trams would comfortably seat thirtytwo persons inside and out although, the announcements of the time record, they could be made to carry double that number by 'dint of squeezing' (to the envy of the present day traffic managers). The roof of the tram was covered with the best quality canvas, well soaked with paint so as to render it thoroughly waterproof, and over this the flooring of the roof was covered with a wooden platform with open type seats which could be kept reasonably dry.

The interior of the trams and furnishings generally were of the kind associated with solid Victorian comfort. There were sliding doors at each end with glass in the upper part of the American ash frames, and at each end the lamps were so placed as to give full light inside and to act as a signal outside. The seats which ran longitudinally were covered with Utrecht velvet and were stuffed with horse-hair, the backs of the seats being panelled and French polished. The windows were glazed with extra quality plate glass, the spaces between the windows being decorated with landscape scenery enclosed in a gilt moulding.

The trams were normally drawn by two horses as the cars were somewhat lighter than the usual run of tramcars. A number of trace-horses were however kept in readiness for use on hills when the occasion required them. The company had at the outset sixty horses and these were kept in stables at the top of Colston Street.

After the official opening at mid-day on the 9 August 1875, the first fare-paying passengers were carried that afternoon and there was considerable competition among the local populace to obtain seats or even standing room in the new vehicles. It is recorded by the Victorian chronicler that many people 'from the industrial classes' were among the first passengers. The service was maintained up and down without intermission for the rest of the day and the waiting queues – as in the evening peak hours of today – never seemed to grow any less. In the course of the afternoon peals were rung on the bells of St Michael's Church in celebration of the event.

The undertaking was a success from the start. The company proceeded in the next few years to increase its capital and to construct further tramways in Bristol, so that by 1881 services were also being run through Victoria Street to Bath Bridge, from St Augustine's Place to Hotwells, from Bristol Bridge to Mill Lane, Bedminster, from the Horsefair to Horfield, and through Bath Street and Tower Hill to Old Market Street.

In 1880 the company – never lacking in enterprise –

experimented with a steam tram which was of somewhat ungainly appearance. This ran for nearly a year on the Horfield line, but the engine proved uneconomical to the company as well as being noisy and unpleasant for the passengers and the horse trams were brought back.

The company's carriage department first appeared in July 1886 as a separate concern under the name of the Bristol Cab Company Ltd. The majority of the local cab and carriage firms had been bought up and the new company announced its aims in the following prospectus:

'It is well known that the Bristol cab service has in the past been inefficiently conducted, the charges having been excessive and there has been a lack of discipline among the men. Much of this has doubtless arisen from the fact that the drivers, being paid only nominal wages, were forced to adopt a system of overcharge and demands for fees, which has been carried to such an extent as to make the hiring of a cab distasteful to a large portion of the public, especially ladies. A passenger who hires a company's cab may rest assured that these defects have been remedied.'

In the following year, 1887, the two concerns were amalgamated under the title of the Bristol Tramways & Carriage Company Limited.

Then came an era of great expansion and development in both departments. On the carriage side the company built up a large fleet of cabs, broughams, landaus, victorias, wedding carriages, four-in-hand drags, wagonettes and even dog carts and bath chairs. It carried the city's mails; it ran livery stables and riding stables; it operated commercial vehicles and acted as general horsing contractors. And lastly — in more than one sense of that word — it provided the funeral equipages. Thus did the Tramway Company justify its claim to look after the Bristolian from the cradle to the grave. Seldom can there have been so complete and varied a transport system in the control of one undertaking.

During the last decade of the nineteenth century the tramway department was also making spectacular progress. The company had noticed with great interest the experiment in electric traction at Leeds in 1891 and being satisfied that the new method of operation gave greater economy, reliability and speed, it decided to adopt an electric system in the proposed Kingswood extension. Once again the company had to go through a lengthy period of negotiations, applications and other formalities, but this time it had the full support of the Bristol Corporation and of the local boards of Kingswood and St George. On 14 October 1895 the electric tramway between Old Market and Kingswood was ceremoniously opened and Bristol became the first town in the country to adopt this method of operation for regular and continuous services (the lines at Leeds and Walsall being only experimental). Public interest could hardly be restrained, as may be judged from a contemporary description of the first trial run:

'So keen were the residents on the subject of electric traction that some circumspection was needed in order to make the first run in comparative quiet. It was made shortly after midnight. The good people of Bristol had scarce entered into their first sleep when a glaring light streaked across the bedroom windows. They realised that the company were stealing a march on them; up went windows and out went heads and there was the first car gliding down the street. That part of Bristol which was traversed by the electric cars immediately got up and waited for the return of the surreptitious car. Never was an electric car awaited in this country by a scantier-clad concourse.'

The company at once initiated a great extension of electrical working and the construction of new lines. Considerable controversy still raged in certain parts of the city, whilst in Clifton the opposition led to the withdrawal of lines projected in that district. By 1897, a second line — between Old Market and Eastville — had been electrified, leaving seven lines still to be worked by horses. By 1900, however, the whole system had been converted to electric traction.

Meanwhile another operating development was taking place — the emergence of the bus. The first horse-buses had appeared in Bristol in 1877 as a feeder to the tram terminus at St George, but this ancillary service was withdrawn when the tramway was extended. The first regular horse-bus service was that operated between the Centre and the Clifton Suspension Bridge from 1881 onwards, but it was not until well into the Edwardian era — when the motor bus appeared — that there was any serious rival to the blue trams.

Enough has probably been said to explain the tremendous importance of the transport revolution in Bristol in the nineteenth century. The quick and efficient tramway contributed in no small part to the rapid expansion of the city from a population of some 100,000 in 1800 to a population of well over 300,000 in 1900. And the influence of Bristol's transport was nationwide; since both the horse tramway system and the electric tramway system were pioneered in the city. The horses have gone. And so have the cabs, the carriages, the funeral carriages and all those other picturesque vehicles of the Victorian era. The trams disappeared in the last war. And even the blue livery is now only a memory; But something remains — something intangible — which makes the Bristol public still look to the 'Tramway Company', still talk about the blue taxis, and still forgive the errors and omissions of service which can hardly be avoided in the very different conditions of today.

I can only hope that you have derived some enjoyment from this account of another age. In the present day when mechanical transport takes us faster and faster not only in the vicinity of our homes, but also further and further afield, it is perhaps pleasant to remember the more leisurely days when man was dependent upon the horse. It may even be more consolation to the transport officials of today to realise that our predecessors in Victorian times had their problems too. It may sound easy to have to deal only with horses, to be comparatively free of engineers (if not of accountants), and to have a well nigh unlimited supply of cheap labour. But there are worries other than economic problems and there are anxieties other than those caused by manpower shortage and staff disputes. And who is to say which are the most exacting?

EARLY OMNIBUS SERVICES IN BIRMINGHAM, 1834-1905

Alec G. Jenson

This paper was issued by the Omnibus Society as part of its 'additional publications scheme'. Mr Jenson, who is President of the Birmingham Transport Historical Group, would welcome any additional information, photographs or tickets related to early omnibus and tramway companies in Birmingham, to forward the Group's researches. They may be sent to him care of the Omnibus Society.

The date of the first omnibus in Birmingham has frequently been quoted as 1828, that is, a year before Shillibeer's venture in London, and the name of the operator as John Doughty. This date has for some time been suspect because in spite of Birmingham's motto 'Forward', it would seem hardly likely in the circumstances that omnibuses would have been running in Birmingham before Shillibeer's London experiment. The error probably originated in a letter published in the *Birmingham Weekly Post* in 1878 when a correspondent stated that his 'recollection' of the first omnibus was that it ran in 1828 and 'it was started by an old man, a Mr Doughty, fishmonger, of High Street.'

Further research, however, has revealed a short paragraph in one only of the three principal Birmingham newspapers of that time which establishes the date as being Monday, 5 May 1834. The paragraph is quaintly worded and reads as follows:

'An omnibus commenced running for the first time in this town, on Monday se'night. Its route is from the Swan, Snowhill, through the town, by way of Bull-street, High-street, Worcester-street, Smallbrook-street, and along the

Bristol-road, to the first turnpike gate. It performs four journies to and fro in the course of the day.'

Birmingham Advertiser, 15 May 1834

The service was run by John Smith of the Malt Shovel Inn, Smallbrook Street, and the first timetable was published on 12 May 1834, showing four journeys each way on weekdays and three on Sundays:

'JOHN SMITH, Malt Shovel Inn, Smallbrook-street, respectfully informs the Ladies and Gentlemen of Birmingham, that he has now regulated the time of departure of his OMNIBUS, which he commenced running a few days ago, and begs to solicit their kind support.

LEAVES		LEAVES	
Smallbrook-street	½ past 8	Edgbaston	¼ before 9
Snow-hill	¼ before 11		½ past 11
	¼ past 11		at 2
	at 4		¼ past 4
	at 6		½ past 6

ON SUNDAYS

LEAVES		LEAVES	
Smallbrook-street	at 10	Edgbaston	¼ past 10
Snow-hill	¼ before 1		½ past 1
	½ past 5		at 6
	at 8		½ past 8

May 8, 1834'   *Aris's Gazette,* 12 May, 1834

Two months later two new routes were commenced by W. Doughty, one to Five Ways, Edgbaston and the other to the Beehive near Handsworth turnpike, both from the White Horse, Steelhouse Lane.

At the end of the year J. Doughty was advertising a named omnibus — the *Favourite* — to Dudley from St George's Tavern, High Street, Birmingham, and in 1835 he started an additional route to Wolverhampton.

The omnibus appears to have been classed legally as a 'short stage carriage' and as such was not supposed to stand in the streets. This accounts for the fact that omnibuses were advertised as starting from inns or taverns in the same way as stage coaches. Further, omnibuses were prohibited from picking up or setting down passengers in the streets, but after the passing of an Act in 1832 this practice, which had developed owing to the nature of the service, became legal.

TWO EARLY OMNIBUS COMPANIES IN BIRMINGHAM

Two omnibus companies were formed in 1836 to develop the traffic on the main roads through West Bromwich to Wolverhampton and Dudley respectively. The first was the Birmingham Omnibus Conveyance Company, floated in January 1836 with a capital of £5,000. A service from Birmingham to West Bromwich was inaugurated and this was subsequently extended to both Wolverhampton and Dudley. The second and rival company was the Midland Omnibus Company, which issued a prospectus in August 1836 offering shares to raise a capital of £15,000.

Apparently omnibus drivers and conductors at this early date were guilty of misconduct and had become the subject of complaints from the travelling public, as in the Midland Company's prospectus the following statement occurs:

'The glaring misconduct of both drivers and conductors together with the terrifying effect and often fatal consequences arising from careless and furious driving, prevent many (especially females) from availing themselves of those facilities which, otherwise, they might feel desirous to embrace...'

The Midland Omnibus Company purchased the businesses of both Doughty and Hughes and thus secured the services on the Wolverhampton, Dudley and Stourbridge routes, as well as the local service along Hagley Road hitherto operated by Hughes. A dispute arose between the two companies over the purchase of Smith's Bristol Road omnibus and an announcement appeared in the local papers in November 1836 to the effect that the Midland Omnibus Company would withdraw from that route.

One of the earliest examples of co-ordination of road and railway services occurred in Birmingham during the period

BIRMINGHAM'S OMNIBUSES

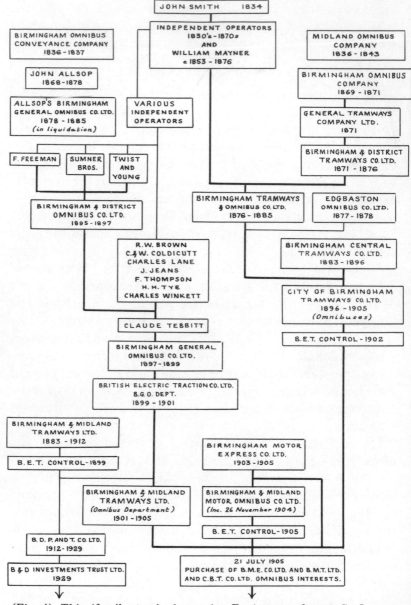

(Fig 4) This 'family tree', drawn by E. Axten, after A.G. Jenson, illustrates the evolution of the Birmingham and Midland Motor Omnibus Company Ltd *(Midland Red)* as the dominant operator in the city

between the opening of the temporary terminus of the Grand Junction Railway at Vauxhall in 1837 and the extension to New Street in 1854. The Midland Omnibus Company advertised a service of omnibuses from their office at 66 High Street to connect with the trains.

The Conveyance Company's advertisements in the local papers ceased about 1837, but the Midland Company's timetables appeared in Wrightson & Webb's Directory until 1843.

OMNIBUS PROPRIETORS IN THE 1840s AND 50s

During this period, omnibus services were advertised in local directories to towns as far afield as Kidderminster, Redditch, Studley, Bromsgrove, Solihull, Coleshill and Tamworth. It may be surmised that these services were worked into Birmingham by outside proprietors owing to the fact that the timings showed the omnibuses leaving Birmingham in the late afternoon and early evening.

Local suburban services were being established in the early '40s, as Wrightson & Webb's Directory for 1846 lists the following routes:

OMNIBUSES
PAGE'S OMNIBUS TO AND FROM SMETHWICK AND SPON LANE
From the Grand Turk, Bell Street, Birmingham
To Spon Lane, West Bromwich
Three times daily.
MOSELEY, BALSALL HEATH, HIGHGATE AND CAMP HILL OMNIBUS
To Moseley and Balsall Heath
Six times daily on Weekdays
Four times on Sundays
From Swan Coach Office, New Street.
NEW STREET AND EDGBASTON OMNIBUS
From Swan Coach Office
To Plough & Harrow, Edgbaston
One daily and from

Top of New Street
  Five times daily
  Six journeys from the Plough & Harrow.
HARBORNE OMNIBUS
  From Bee Hive, Bull Street
  To New Inn, Harborne
    Five times daily on Weekdays
    Four times on Sundays.
BRISTOL ROAD OMNIBUS
  From Bee Hive, Bull Street
  To Toll-gate, Bristol Road
    Six times daily on Weekdays
    Twice on Sundays.
HANDSWORTH OMNIBUS THROUGH HUNTER'S LANE
  From Rose & Punch Bowl, Bull Street
  To Frighted Horse and New Inn, Handsworth
    Seven times daily.

Some of the early pioneers who helped to establish the services on the main roads out of Birmingham are remembered as local characters:

Perrin was operating on Hagley Road in 1841-2 but was unable to make the service a paying proposition and in the early 1850s was working to Harborne and then on the Handsworth route jointly with William Mayner. His interest in the latter route passed to Tolley in the late 50s.

Joseph Brookes, in later years the owner of a large coach establishment in Hurst Street, started an omnibus service on Bristol Road in 1846 and after a gap of some years was again operating this route in 1862 in partnership under the name of Sheppard, Brookes and Oakes.

Hughes commenced running to Moseley in 1846, presumably after selling his rights on Hagley Road to the Midland Omnibus Company, and may have been the operator of the Highgate, Camp Hill and Moseley Omnibus referred to above.

William Mayner was a noted character; he was a rogue convicted and sentenced to five years penal servitude at the

Warwick assizes in 1855 for receiving stolen property. He resumed his business as an omnibus proprietor on the Handsworth and Lozells routes and during this period was prosecuted for causing obstruction at the Heathfield Road terminus by allowing his horses to stand in the roadway. He was fined on another occasion in a case of assault involving a passenger on one of the rival omnibuses operated by his son William Mayner Junior, as apparently considerable ill feeling existed between the father and son.

Bennett, an Edgbaston operator, inaugurated one of the earliest cross town routes from the Plough & Harrow, Hagley Road, to Bloomsbury, but this facility was later discontinued and such cross town services have never been an important feature of Birmingham's transport system.

One of the earliest examples of a special or excursion working occurs in a footnote to the timetable of the Bristol Road omnibus in Showell's Birmingham Almanac for 1848 which reads:

'That during the Strawberry season this omnibus will make two journeys to Strawberry Vale, viz, half-past four, a quarter before seven.'

The Strawberry Vale was a garden in Hall Hill Road (now Edgbaston Park Road) privately owned by a Mrs Wilmore, but open to the public on payment of 1s, 'the value of which could be had in strawberries or flowers.'

Turner acquired the Harbourne (sic) service in 1849 and later a rival operator, Taylor, appeared on the road. The two operators competed with each other for some years and eventually entered either into partnership or working agreement.

Among other well-known names was the Chapman family — father and son — who were so well respected by the public and their passengers that Chapman Senior was presented with an omnibus and horses by the residents of Nechells and Saltley.

Thomas Chapman Senior started the Nechells route in the 1850s and his son later worked the Yardley route and finally ran his omnibuses to Alum Rock.

William Sheppard, originally the owner of the Swan with Two Necks, Aston Street, started an omnibus service to Sutton Coldfield in 1853 and in 1862 he was also operating on Bristol Road in partnership as Sheppard, Brookes & Oakes. In 1864 he opened a branch of his business as omnibus, cab and car proprietor at King's Heath and operated a service of omnibuses to Alcester Lane's End from the Lamp in Bull Street. He advertised in the local directories and timetables.

Heath started the Coventry Road route with a service as far as Muntz Street, Small Heath, in the 1860s and later extended to Yardley.

Abraham Whitehouse operated on Stratford Road, at first as far as the toll gate at the Mermaid (at the junction of Warwick Road and Stratford Road). One of his drivers, Sam Muckley, was a well-known worthy remembered by many, and by one nonagenarian (as recently as 1949) who recounted that as a boy travelling daily to King Edward's School it was his ambition to sit on the box to listen to Sam Mucklow's stories.

By the end of the 1850s, the principle of omnibus operation in Birmingham had been established with an individual owner working on one or more of each of the main roads out of the town. There were changes of ownership from time to time and combinations of operators working either by agreement or in partnership. Omnibuses have always been under police control and at this period there were the usual prosecutions for overcrowding, furious driving, drunkenness, assault etc, and one amusing letter to the press complained about overcrowding and the practice of passengers accommodating the fair sex by taking them on their knees. The writer, obviously male, was ungallant enough to say that so long as this extended only to the young and pretty they would not have murmured, but elderly dowagers and weighty widows had been pressed upon their notice and this they did not like.

The Town Police Clauses Act became law in 1847 and enabled local authorities to incorporate clauses or sections applying to hackney carriages (which also included omnibuses) in any General Act which might be subsequently promoted. Such acts were referred to as Special Acts and it is in one of these acts, the Birmingham Corporation (Consolidation) Act 1883, that the first mention of omnibuses was made, when the corporation was granted powers to fix standing and starting places, for omnibuses, to issue licences and to make bye-laws in respect of omnibuses.

The Birmingham authorities exercised strict control over the vehicles, condition of the horses, behaviour of the drivers and conductors, and later were granted powers to specify authorised streets along which omnibuses could travel and the times at which they should depart from the termini. This control was exercised at first through the Watch Committee, and in the late 1880s this and other routine work was delegated to the Judicial Sub-Committee which reported to the former committee. An early minute in the Watch Committee's records for 1858 refers to a memorial from the omnibus proprietors requesting permission to stay for ten minutes between the time of their arrival and departure at the terminus. It was agreed, after negotiation, that five minutes should be sufficient time for taking up and setting down passengers.

THE BIRMINGHAM OMNIBUS COMPANY — 1869

A new company, the first for over thirty years was formed under the above title in 1869 with William & Daniel Busby of Liverpool as two of the directors. A fleet of ten green omnibuses built by Miller of London 'on the Paris Plan,' seating fifteen inside and eighteen outside, was advertised to be placed in service on Wednesday, 2 June 1869 on the Hagley Road, Handsworth, Bristol Road, Moseley and Ashton Park routes respectively, following a parade of the new omnibuses through the main streets on the day before. A half-hourly service was provided from the town terminus at the company's 'station' at 53 High Street, where a waiting room and parcel office was provided. Through booking arrangements were also inaugurated from one suburban terminus to another, allowing a change of vehicle

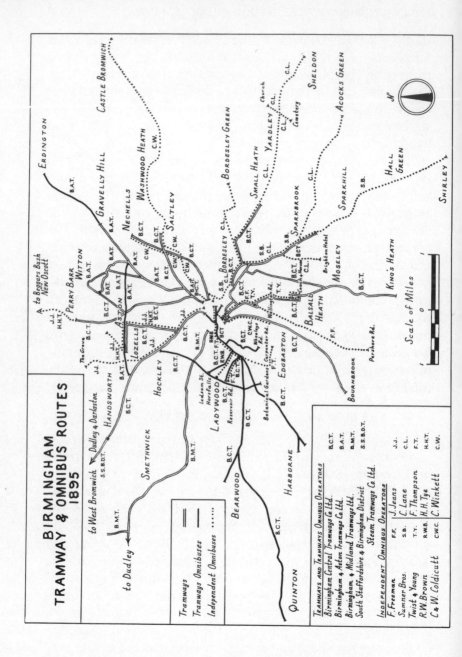

(Fig 5) Map of Birmingham services. Drawn by E. Axten, after A.G. Jenson

at the central office, and discount tickets were also available for regular passengers at a 10 per cent reduction. Kelly's Directory for 1871 lists additional services to those mentioned above to Bloomsbury, King's Heath, Pershore Road and Balsall Heath, Saltley and Small Heath but excludes Harborne Road.

In addition to these services, ten of the original individual operators were still running.

TRAMWAYS

The first tramway proposal was made by George Francis Train in the early 1860s, but owing to lack of capital the venture was abortive.

The Busby syndicate then registered the General Tramways Co Ltd in 1871, but as the prospectus mentioned foreign interests in Lisbon, Saragossa, Madrid and North Italy, this company also failed to attract sufficient capital, with the result that the name was changed to the Birmingham and District Tramways Co Ltd and the foreign interests were excluded. The objects of the company were to operate tramways and to purchase the Birmingham Omnibus Company's business. The first tramway to be opened was the section from Hockley Brook (the Birmingham boundary) to West Bromwich and Dudley Port on which a service of double-deck horse trams were inaugurated on 20 May 1872. It might be presumed that the company were by this time operating the remaining horse omnibus services of the Birmingham Omnibus Company, covering road between Hockley and the centre of Birmingham.*

The tramway was not a financial success and within a few years the company was in liquidation. It is probable that the cause of this was omnibus competition on the Birmingham-

* Under the Tramways Act, 1870 local authorities were empowered to lay down the tramways which they leased to operating companies as an alternative to allowing the companies to lay (and own) the track. The Birmingham Council elected to proceed in this way and when they had laid the track from the borough boundary at Hockley to Monmouth Street (later renamed Colmore Road) they granted the Tramway Company a lease, and the service was extended to Monmouth Street on 11 September 1873.

Handsworth section of the route by William Mayner. A new company was therefore incorporated on 20 May 1876, entitled the Birmingham Tramways & Omnibus Co Ltd with the objects of purchasing the old Tramways Company and also the omnibus business of William Mayner. The new company thus acquired certain omnibus routes; not only those previously operated by the Birmingham Omnibus Company, but also those of William Mayner to Villa Cross and Handsworth. This company also operated the Bristol Road tramway, and for a time a connection was made between the two routes at the Town Hall. It was originally intended to operate a through service between Handsworth and Bournbrook.

The 1883 issue of the Birmingham ABC Railway Timetable lists the following omnibus routes operated by the tramway company:

Colmore Row to Villa Cross
     Heathfield Road via Wheeler Street
     Birchfield
     Wilton via Summer Lane
High Street to Balsall Heath
New Street to Pershore Road
     Edgbaston (St George's Church) via Bristol
     Street, Gough Road and Carpenter Road
     Hagley Road (Hermitage Road).

Two new omnibus companies were incorporated in the late 1870s. The first was the Edgbaston Omnibus Co Ltd, incorporated on 28 June 1877 for the purpose of operating omnibuses, and to develop a machine invented by Mr Russell Brandsby 'for checking the specific distance travelled by passengers in omnibuses and other public conveyances.' This company operated a half-hourly service of omnibuses from the Swan office, New Street, to Hagley Road, but the omnibus part of the undertaking was sold to the tramways company in 1878.

The second company was the floating of a business hitherto conducted by Benjamin John Allsop who had been operating omnibuses between Aston and the centre of Birmingham from 1868. The company was named Allsop's Birmingham General Omnibus Co Ltd, and was incorporated on 29 April 1878. Allsop remained manager of the undertaking and later in the same year the business owned by William Taylor (formerly Turner & Taylor) of Harborne was purchased, and Allsops then ran omnibuses on the Harborne Road. Allsop's services, according to the March 1883 issue of the Birmingham ABC Railway Timetables were as follows:

New Street to Victoria Road via Aston New Town
       Nechells (Villa Tavern)
       Hagley Road (Manor Road) jointly with the
        Birmingham Tramways & Omnibus Co Ltd
       Harborne
High Street to Aston Park and Lower Grounds
       Gravelly Hill and Erdington
Aston Park to Hagley Road (Hermitage Road) a cross town
      service.

Allsop's was the first undertaking to introduce penny fares which they did on the Aston Road route in 1882. The company went into liquidation in 1885, probably owing to tramway competition, and the assets were sold to the Birmingham Cab Company.

STEAM TRAMWAYS

The steam tramway engine was developed in spite of strict Board of Trade regulations during the late 70s and early 80s, and Birmingham and the Black Country eventually possessed the largest network of steam tramways in the country.

The first line was opened on 26 December 1882 by the Birmingham & Aston Tramways Co Ltd from the Old Square, Birmingham to Witton via Aston Cross. A branch to Gravelly Hill was opened for traffic in 1885.

Owing to the fact that Allsop's had ceased to operate omnibuses, there was, in 1885, no means of road transport between Gravelly Hill and Erdington. The tramway company therefore commenced a service of omnibuses as a feeder to the tramway from the terminus at Gravelly Hill to Erdington.

The omnibuses were timed to connect with the trams. A second omnibus service between Lichfield Road (The Vine) and Handsworth via Victoria Road and Lozells Road was inaugurated by the tramway company in December 1894. This route was the forerunner of the only inter-suburban tram route not serving the centre of the city.

A comprehensive scheme for tramways in Birmingham was developed between the years 1884 and 1886 and the Birmingham Central Tramways Co Ltd were operating steam trams on many of the main roads by 1886. The Birmingham Corporation constructed the track which was leased to the tramway companies for operation. The Central Company operated services to Perry Barr, Saltley, Small Heath, Sparkbrook, Moseley and King's Heath via Balsall Heath. Nechells was at first worked by steam trams and subsequently with horse trams.

This development necessitated the purchase in some cases of omnibuses working on services which would compete with the trams and it is recorded that Charles Lane's service on the Stratford Road and Allsop's services in the Aston and Nechells districts were purchased in this way.

During 1885 the financial affairs of the Birmingham Tramways & Omnibus Co Ltd were unsatisfactory and the Birmingham Central Tramways Co Ltd agreed to purchase the undertaking. This purchase was completed on 8 December 1885 and the following omnibus routes passed to the Central Company.

Colmore Row to Birchfield via Summer Lane
                 Browne's Green
                 Handsworth (Villa Cross)
                 Heathfield Road via Wheeler Street
New Street to Bearwood (Cock and Magpie)
                 Pershore Road
Albert Street to Moseley.

The Birmingham Central Tramways Co Ltd developed their omnibus services between the years 1885 and 1894, during which period the following routes were started:

New Street to Harborne (possibly after the withdrawal of
Allsop's omnibuses)
Colmore Row to Five Ways, Edgbaston
New Street to Bearwood (Bear Inn) via Hagley Road
Edgbaston (Botanical Gardens) to Hockley Brook
New Street to Quinton
> Ledsam Street via Ryland Street
> Wheeleys Road via Granville Street
> Reservoir Road via Ladywood Road

Some of the original routes were later discontinued and
were worked by independent operators.

Special vehicles were also run to football matches and to
the County Ground in Edgbaston Road with charabancs and
omnibuses by the Tramway Company and other independent
operators.

The traffic on the Handsworth 4ft 8½in gauge tramway was
sufficient to justify conversion to 3ft 6in gauge cable operation, the work being completed between 1888 to 1889.
During reconstruction of the track the service was maintained
with omnibuses. The Bristol Road route, also worked by
horse trams on the standard gauge, was reconstructed to the
3ft 6in gauge and a service of electric accumulator trams
commenced on 25 July 1890. Horse omnibuses were also
used on this route during the period of reconstruction.

AMALGAMATION OF THE REMAINING OMNIBUS INTERESTS

The tramways proved to be a serious competitor of the omnibuses and in an endeavour to maintain some of the established
routes the Birmingham & District Omnibus Co Ltd was incorporated on 17 September 1895 for the purpose of acquiring
the following firms of omnibus operators and their routes:

Twist & Young   - New Street to Balsall Heath
Frederick Freeman - New Street to Pershore Road
Sumner Brothers   - High Street to Shirley.

The company was in financial difficulties in less than two
years and at an extraordinary meeting held on 18 February
1897, approval was given for the sale of the business to

one Claude Tebbitt. Claude Tebbitt was presumably an intermediary as this sale was followed by the incorporation of the Birmingham General Omnibus Co Ltd on 3 April 1897 to acquire from Claude Tebbitt the business, property and routes of the Birmingham & District Omnibus Co Ltd, and in addition those of the following independent operators:

C. & W.Coldicutt - New Street to Wellington Road, via
                  Bristol Street
Charles Winkett - Dale End to Nechells
                  Dale End to Castle Bromwich
H.H. Tye   - Colmore Row to Heathfield Road, via
                  Wheeler Street
J. Jeans   - Colmore Row to Heathfield Road, via
                  Wheeler Street
                  Colmore Row to Browne's Green
                  Perry Bar to Oscott (Beggar's Bush)
F. Thompson   - New Street to Ladywood Road
                  New Street to Carpenter Road
R.W. Brown   - New Street to Monument Road, via
                  Ryland Street
Charles Lane   - High Street to Yardley and Sheldon
                  High Street to Bordesley Green
                  High Street to Ladypool Road
                  High Street to Acocks Green

Unfortunately history once again repeated itself as the new company was unable to make the business pay. It went into liquidation in September 1899 and the assets were purchased by the British Electric Traction Co Ltd.

Meanwhile the Birmingham Central Tramways Co Ltd had been approached by a syndicate sponsored by two Canadians, William Mackenzie, President of the Toronto Street Tramways and James Ross, Managing Director of the Montreal Tramways Company, with a proposition to acquire the Birmingham tramways and to equip them for electric operation, on condition that the corporation would grant them an extension of the existing leases. This offer was accepted by the company and the tramway and omnibus undertaking passed to a new company, the City of Birmingham Tramways Co Ltd incorporated on 29 September 1896.

Unfortunately the company and the corporation were unable to agree on the question of terms for the conversion of the tramways, and in November 1899 the Birmingham City Council resolved that no further leases would be granted within the city and that upon the expiry of those existing they would work the tramways themselves. In spite of this decision the company proceeded with the conversion of some of the tramways to overhead electric traction, the first being the Bristol Road route which was opened for service on 13 May 1901. The British Electric Traction Co Ltd then made an offer to purchase a controlling interest in the company and Mr James Ross accepted, agreed to the sale of his shares, and at the same time secured for his fellow shareholders the right to sell at the same price for 37s 6d cum dividend per share. The sale was reported in the *Tramway and Railway World* dated 10 July 1902.

THE BRITISH ELECTRIC TRACTION CO LTD

The British Electric Traction Co Ltd, incorporated in 1896 for the purpose of developing electric tramways in various parts of the British Isles, thus had two groups of omnibus services in Birmingham operated by two separate undertakings. Negotiations were then opened for the purchase of the five tramway companies operating in the area between Birmingham and Wolverhampton known as the Black Country. A controlling interest was obtained in the Birmingham & Midland Tramways Ltd in 1901. This company operated the steam tramway from Birmingham to Oldbury and Dudley with two branches to West Bromwich from West Smethwick and Oldbury respectively. The latter two routes were at that time being operated as shuttle services under lease by Crowther, an undertaker of West Bromwich, with single-deck horse trams. It was decided by the BET Co Ltd, to transfer to this company the omnibus business purchased from the Birmingham General Omnibus Co Ltd in 1899 and which had been operated since that date as the Birmingham General Omnibus Department of the BET Co Ltd under Mr J.W. Tobutt as Chief Inspector. This transfer was done by way of sale to the Birmingham & Midland Tramways Ltd, the date of completion being 31 December 1901, after which date the omnibus undertaking became the Omnibus Department of the tramway company.

CONTROL OF OMNIBUS OPERATION
BY THE JUDICIAL SUB-COMMITTEE

This Sub-committee was appointed during the 1880s to advise and assist the Watch Committee, among other duties, on day to day matters concerning omnibus operation, and the control exercised was extremely strict. For instance operators were not allowed to commence a new route, to vary a route, alter a timetable or even to run additional or withdraw omnibuses without the prior approval of the sub-committee. Occasionally, however, the Chief Constable would permit a minor route variation pending the sub-committee's approval. The vehicles were examined and licensed annually by the Hackney Carriage Inspector and operators were liable to be fined if they worked an unlicensed vehicle. Many matters which would be regarded today of minor importance occupied a considerable amount of the sub-committee's time. In 1890-1 a Mr Bragg of Handsworth complained about the omnibus windows being obscured by advertisements, a matter upon which the Town Clerk was called upon to advise. In 1893 there was friction between the Police and the time-keeper employed by Twist & Young at the Balsall Heath terminus, and in April of that year the Hackney Carriage Inspector was instructed to warn omnibus proprietors that if vehicles were not submitted for inspection at the place and time specified in the notice they would not be allowed to use the vehicles concerned until they had been inspected.

During the years 1893-5 permission was granted for the following new services (the dates given are those of the meeting at which such approval was granted and *not* the commencement of the service):

8 May 1893   Fred Thompson, a single horse omnibus — New Street to the junction of Ladywood Road and Monument Road via Ladywood Road.

12 June 1893 Birmingham Central Tramways Co Ltd — New Street to the junction of Ledsam Street and Monument Road via Ryland Street.

Permission was also granted for a brake to pick up passengers at Five Ways and along Calthorpe Road, Priory Road and Edgbaston Road en route for the County cricket ground and vice versa.

10 July 1893   Frederick Freeman — St Martin's Lane to corner of Ladypool Road and Brighton Road.

22 Sept 1893 Birmingham Central Tramways Co Ltd — New Street to corner of Wheeleys Road and St James' Road via Granville Street, William Street and George Road.

7 May 1894   William Gwillym - Wheeler Street route.

In 1893 revised hackney carriage and omnibus bye-laws were under consideration and one of the most important provisions was the granting of powers to the local authority 'to specify the time of starting and route by which each and every stage carriage shall convey passengers within the boundaries of the city.' Two years later when the Hackney Carriage Inspector visited Scotland Yard to investigate the workings of omnibuses and cabs in London, he found that the police there had no powers to restrict the number of vehicles plying for hire nor to specify routes and he was advised by the Superintendent of the Public Carriage Department of Scotland Yard to recommend adoption of the proposal to limit the number of omnibuses and to specify the routes in Birmingham. When the bye-laws came into operation in December 1896 a revised list of authorised routes was included.

During the period 1898 to 1902, the minutes of the Judicial Sub-committee record a considerable amount of historical detail, such as opening of new routes, transfer of licences and other items connected with the day to day operation of the services. For instance it is recorded that at a meeting held on 25 July 1898 the Birmingham General Omnibus Co Ltd was granted permission to operate a new service of omnibuses from New Street to St George's Church, Edgbaston, and at a meeting on 12 December of the same year the first application to run motor omnibuses was recommended for approval.

In July 1899 the Chief Constable reported upon the traffic congestion in Old Square which resulted in a proposal to alter the lay-out of the tram terminus in the form of a loop encircling the square. This involved the diversion of chara-bancs, omnibuses and other vehicles catering for football traffic, from Old Square to a loading point in Steelhouse Lane. This proposal caused concern among the operators, and the revised arrangements were only agreed after discussion with a deputation from the Birmingham Vehicle Owners Association. Even then some proprietors were threatened with prosecution for loading at the old terminus, but the Magistrate's Clerk had to advise that no case could be held against them as the notice of removal of the terminus had not been advertised properly and in any case it was not legally worded. This was rectified by the issue of a notice in the local press signed by the Town Clerk.

Information as to the density of omnibus traffic in Birmingham may be obtained from the sub-committee's minutes. The Lord Mayor complained about omnibus congestion at Five Ways, Edgbaston in June 1900, which resulted in a re-arrangement of the stopping places. Before this was decided upon the chief constable had reported that fiftyone omnibuses per hour stopped outside the Five Ways Tavern en route for the city, or nearly one per minute. This total was made up as follows:

From Hagley Road	16 omnibuses
Harborne	9 omnibuses
Carpenter Road	2 omnibuses

From Ladywood Road	4 omnibuses
Starting at Five Ways	20 omnibuses
of which 4 ran to Colmore Row	

In New Street sixtyfour omnibuses per hour turned round:

To Hagley Road	16 omnibuses
Harborne	9 omnibuses
Carpenter Road	2 omnibuses
Five Ways	16 omnibuses
Ladywood Road	4 omnibuses
Ryland Street	6 omnibuses
Bristol Road	8 omnibuses
Pershore Road	3 omnibuses

In October 1900 the committee solemnly deliberated upon the position of destination boards. The bye-laws laid down that omnibuses had to show the destination in a conspicuous position and the chief constable reported that in his opinion the boards should be placed on the front and rear of the vehicle. The first suggestion was that the front board should be exhibited beneath the driver's footboard but it was then realised that in wet weather it would be hidden by the driver's apron! The British Electric Traction Co Ltd adopted the principle of painting the destination on the panels on each side of the driver, and in addition had a removable board fixed above the advertising space at the top of the rear of their vehicles. This arrangement limited the use of the omnibuses to the routes to which they were allocated but as the addition of an extra vehicle needed prior approval of the sub-committee this was presumably not a serious drawback. The City of Birmingham Tramways Co Ltd, on the other hand, had let their front panels for advertising and the boards therefore were placed in brackets above the panels.

The same minute records that four other 'small' omnibus proprietors were notified of the manner in which destination boards should be fixed. These proprietors were probably Thomas Chapman Junior operating to Alum Rock, his partner Frederick Freeman operating also to Alum Rock as well as to Washwood Heath, G.R. Lane working to Yardley, and possibly

William Wall who it was stated 'worked on Broad Street at busy times.' Chapman and Freeman shortly after this decided to dissolve partnership and executed an agreement between themselves relating to the operation of the routes concerned. When this was brought to the notice of the sub-committee, they were informed in no uncertain terms that the committee was the only authority to decide who should be granted permission to run and they were both instructed by the chief constable to attend the committee meeting to clear up the matter. It was decided that the Alum Rock service would be jointly operated and that Freeman would run the service to Washwood Heath until such time as a second omnibus was required when this would be provided by Chapman.

Early in 1901, Mr Hugh Thomas applied for, and was granted, a licence to run omnibuses on Pershore Road to Stirchley in competition with the BET Co Ltd's omnibuses on the understanding that the Kings Norton and Northfield UDC would also grant a licence.

During 1901 the chief constable received a complaint about the condition of the horses employed on the Balsall Heath route and he reported to the sub-committee that the cause was a 'skin disease which had run its course through the stables leaving the horses fit for work but presenting a poor and rough appearance.' This complaint may have had some connection with Chapman's misfortune in losing all his horses through a similar disease which caused his own death. His grand-daughter, Miss Elsie M. Chapman, said in a letter that 'My grandfather died in tragic circumstances when I was a small school girl. He was running buses to Saltley and Alum Rock at the time, when a disease broke out in all the stables killing off all his lovely horses and many replacements. Being an animal lover he did all he could, but caught the disease and died.' This is confirmed by a resolution dated 22 April 1901 that the sub-committee approved a proposal that the BET Co Ltd would take over the position held by the late Thomas Chapman and also the two omnibuses. Chapman's character is reflected in a personal note, as my father once told me many years ago that when he was apprenticed to a chemist in Birmingham his parents lived at Yardley. He used to go home on Saturday nights, being allowed to leave the shop early to catch the last bus. (Closing time on Saturdays in those days was midnight.) Chapman was at that time working the Yardley route and occasionally he used to allow my father to ride free.

After acquiring Chapman's buses, the BET Co Ltd combined their Bordesley Green route with the Alum Rock and Wash-wood Heath routes, thus forming cross-city services, and about the same time the Nechells and Ladywood Road and the Ryland Street routes were also combined. One of the old drivers, Mr C. Kendrick, recalls that he drove on this route from Bordesley Green via Coventry Road, Carrs Lane, Dale End (Red Lion) and Saltley to the Fox & Goose, Washwood Heath and at week-ends through to the Bradford Arms, Castle Bromwich.

In July 1901 the chief constable reported to the sub-committee that he had received a letter from Mr Warren, the manager of the City of Birmingham Tramways Co Ltd, intimating that his company had decided to discontinue the omnibus service between Five Ways and Colmore Road. The sub-committee directed that Mr Warren be informed that they were 'surprised to learn that he has discontinued the service referred to without communicating with the chief constable,' which brought in reply a letter of apology from Mr Warren.

In October 1901, the chief constable reported that Mr Fairbairn, the manager of the BET Co Ltd, Birmingham General Omnibus Department, had sent a communication stating that he had been compelled to discontinue the omnibus service to Handsworth Wood owing to inadequate receipts and that the company had sold an omnibus to James Jeans who then applied for and was granted a licence to work the route. At the same meeting permission was granted to the BET Co Ltd to operate a connecting service between Lionel Street and Dale End via New Street at a fare of ½d. The object of this service was to connect the services of the Birmingham

& Midland Tramways Ltd with the centre of the city.

F. Freeman sold his omnibuses to G.R. Lane in November 1901 and the licences were transferred. A long report was necessary when in January 1902 Lane applied for permission to run an extra bus to Alum Rock.

In January 1902 the chief constable received a letter of complaint from the Birmingham & Midland Tramways Ltd referring to the 'recent disturbances'. This was presumably the Lloyd George riots on 18 December 1901, when a number of omnibuses were damaged.

It was in 1902 that the late O. Cecil Power first became connected with Birmingham's omnibus business when he was appointed manager of the Omnibus Department of the Birmingham & Midland Tramways Ltd. He applied for permission to vary the Bordesley Green, Acocks Green and Lady-wood routes, and in April 1903 inaugurated regular Sunday services of omnibuses to Earlswood, Stonebridge and Coles-hill. This was against the opposition of charabanc proprietors who had for many years operated between them seven excursion services on Sunday afternoons (provided they secured a sufficient number of passengers) to Henley-in-Arden, Berks-well, Stonebridge, Earlswood, Coleshill, Meriden and either Castle Bromwich or Knowle. The charabanc proprietors were offered similar facilities by the sub-committee to operate regular services but none of them accepted.

ASTON MANOR OMNIBUS SERVICES

The Urban District Council of Aston Manor instructed Mr R.P. Wilson to report upon the steam tramways then being operated by the Birmingham & Aston Tramways Co Ltd and as the result of his report the council decided to purchase the undertaking under powers included in the Tramways Act 1870, and to convert the whole system, which they proposed extending, to overhead traction. It was decided that after conversion the tramways should be operated by the British Electric Traction Co Ltd through its subsidiary company, the City of Birmingham Tramways Co Ltd. The purchase price was fixed by arbitration and the undertaking passed into council control on 30 June 1902. During the period of conversion the council operated the steam tram services as hitherto as well as the horse omnibus routes between Gravelly Hill and Erdington and between Lichfield Road and Handsworth respectively.

The Aston Manor Council (Municipal Borough 1903) was therefore the first local authority in the Birmingham area actually to operate omnibuses, and further the position was unique in that the one service was entirely outside the borough and in the area of the adjoining Urban District of Erdington.* The *Birmingham Daily Post* for 8 September 1902 records that a motor 'car' service was inaugurated between Salford Bridge (Gravelly Hill) and Erdington by a Mr W.W. Greener and his agent, Mr Edward Allsopp. The vehicle was a 10-seat Daimler.

THE MOTOR OMNIBUS

The Judicial Sub-committee recommended approval of an application by the Llandudno Motor Touring Company to run three motor omnibuses on a route in Birmingham at a meeting on 12 December 1898. This was the first occasion upon which the sub-committee was asked to sanction a motor omnibus service, and the proposed route was from Dale End via Coleshill Street, Great Brook Street, Great Francis Street, Saltley Road, Alum Rock Road, Highfield Road, Washwood Heath Road and Ward End to the Fox & Goose. Representatives of the company attended the meeting and approval was granted on the understanding that:

'the higher gear shall not be used at all in the centre of the city, drivers confining themselves to the second rate of speed — 6 mph,' and:

* The Lichfield Road and Handsworth omnibus service was probably discontinued when the electric trams commenced operation on this route, but the working of the Erdington omnibus service was taken over by the Birmingham & Midland Tramways Joint Committee and operated as the Erdington Omnibus Department until 24 June 1906, when it was discontinued, partly as it was being worked at a loss and partly due to the impending construction of the Erdington tramway.

'the machinery (sic) shall be stopped at the Town Terminus, if the vehicle remains more than two minutes for the purpose of taking up passengers.'

It is not known whether this service ever operated but in April 1900 the chief constable refers in a report to excursions by *motor-cars* and four-in-hand coaches to Stratford-upon-Avon and other places.

At a meeting held on 6 October 1901, the chief constable reported upon an application by Cox & Rooksby of 88 Colmore Row for permission to run a service of motor-cars between the Fountain, Hagley Road and Moseley via Hagley Road, Calthorpe Road, Church Road, Priory Road and Edgbaston Road. It was proposed to charge 1d fare from The Fountain to Five Ways as compared with 2d charged by the City of Birmingham Tramways Co Ltd on their horse omnibuses. The tramway company objected to the terminus at the Fountain, but as they proposed discontinuing the Carpenter Road route the Chief Constable said that he saw no reason why the manager, Mr Warren, should object to the Ivy Bush as the starting point for the service. The application, however, was refused partly on account of the opinion of the sub-committee that the route suggested would not be successful and partly because they felt they must defer granting the licences pending the actual formation and registration of a company.

A further application to run motor omnibuses in the city, received from the Birmingham Motor Express Co Ltd and Mr Olivieri was considered at a meeting on 29 June 1903. This company received the certificate of incorporation dated for the next day, 30 June 1903, and a special sub-committee was appointed to consider the application.

The Chief Constable reported at a meeting on 26 October 1903 that three motor vehicles had been submitted for licences, viz:

No 251   An omnibus built by Messrs Mulliner fitted with 12 hp engine(s) and constructed to carry ten persons inside and two outside (ie by the driver).

Nos 291   Char-a-bancs, built by Messrs Mulliner with 12
& 292   hp Napier engines but constructed to carry
fourteen persons.

A temporary licence was granted and an arrangement made
with the Wolseley Tool & Motor Company to examine and
report upon the 'mechanical portion' of the vehicles at a fee
of five guineas which included the 'capabilities of the driver'
and was payable to the proprietors of the vehicles. Subsequent
examinations would be undertaken for a fee of two guineas.
No fixed timetable was enforced for the first few weeks and
the vehicle commenced operation between New Street and
The Fountain, Hagley Road. It was stipulated that the motor
omnibuses should turn around the refuge at the top of
Worcester Street and stand at the rear of the horse omnibuses
in order to avoid the risk of startling the horses.

At the next meeting held on 23 November 1903, a deputation from the Birmingham Motor Express Co Ltd attended
and stated that six new vehicles had been ordered and were
expected to be ready for delivery early in 1904. These were
to be of Milnes-Daimler manufacture and it was hoped that
the cause for complaint from the authorities of King Edward's
School (presumably from noise) should cease. The Motor Car
Act 1903 came into force on 1 January 1904 and one of the
requirements was the registration of motor vehicles and the
provision of number plates as well as the licensing of drivers.
These duties became part of the work of the Public Carriage
Department. The first (Napier) vehicles therefore went into
service without number plates. The motor omnibuses proved
to be unreliable and frequently broke down on the road and
the company, in an endeavour to find a more suitable make
of vehicle, purchased motor omnibuses of Dürkopp, Wolesley
and Thornycroft manufacture. The services operated with
motor omnibuses were:

New Street to Hagley Road (Fountain) via Broad Street,
Five Ways and Hagley Road.

General Hospital to Harborne (Duke of York) via Corporation Street, Broad Street, Five Ways and Harborne Road.

Both services were in connection with the City of Birmingham Tramways Co Ltd's horse omnibuses.

The Birmingham Motor Express Co Ltd soon needed additional capital and was responsible for the incorporation of the Birmingham & Midland Omnibus Co Ltd on 24 November 1904 which was formed to acquire the Birmingham Motor Express Co Ltd and to take over certain agreements with Milnes-Daimler Ltd for the supply of six omnibuses and others relating to advertising, motor oil and motor spirit. The directors of the new company were: William John Taylor, company director; John Jordan, company director; Thomas Ottery, company director; William Roberts, estate agent; Edward Augustus Olivieri, merchant; John White, Junr, contractor. A capital of £60,000 was authorised but apparently was not subscribed as the public presumably had insufficient confidence in motor omnibuses at that time.

The City of Birmingham Tramways Co Ltd purchased four Dürkopp motor omnibuses in April 1905 with which to meet the competition of the Express Company and these were operated on the Harborne route.

The report of the Birmingham & Midland Motor Omnibus Co Ltd dated 17 June 1905, showed a change in the board of directors which suggests acquisition by the British Electric Traction Co Ltd; the names of Clarence Bayard Shireff Hilton, as Chairman and James Albert Lycett as Managing Director, with Robert Walter Cramp as Traffic Manager and B. Kingsford as Secretary, now appearing with only the name of William Roberts from the old board. The British Electric Traction Co Ltd then decided to amalgamate its omnibus interests in Birmingham and on 21 July 1905 the following company and omnibus undertakings were transferred to the new company by way of sale:

The Birmingham Motor Express Co Ltd	for £30,000
Omnibus Department of the City of Birmingham Tramways Co Ltd	for £42,834
Omnibus Department of the Birmingham & Midland Tramways Ltd	for £77,166

At the same time the capital was increased from £60,000 to £200,000 and Mr O.C. Power was appointed Traffic Manager. The rolling stock, studs, harness and premises taken over included:

Birmingham Motor Express Co Ltd

Motor Omnibuses	6 16/20 hp Milnes-Daimler double-deck 30-seat omnibuses 0-264-269
	9 24 hp Milnes-Daimler double-deck omnibuses 0-1270-78
	1 24 hp Thornycroft double-deck 30-seat omnibus 0-1279
	1 18/20 hp Dürkopp double-deck omnibus 0-1280
	2 20 hp Wolseley double-deck 36-seat omnibuses 0-1281-82
Premises	Garage in Ladywood Road
	Premises at rear of 63 Broad Street

City of Birmingham Tramways Co Ltd

Horse Omnibuses	45
Stud	608 horses including those for 10 tramcars on Nechells route
Motor Omnibuses	4 Dürkopp double-deck omnibus 0-1301-04
Premises	Stables in Bearwood Road
	High Street, Harborne
	Tennant Street, Edgbaston

Birmingham & Midland Tramways Ltd

Horse Omnibuses	74
Stud	510 horses
Premises	Stables in St Mary Street, Ladywood
	Trevor Street, Nechells
	Mary Street, Balsall Heath

Stables in Taunton Road, Sparkbrook
Finch Road, Hands-
worth
Premises in Dale End.

Thus the story of the early omnibus history ends with the final amalgamation of the remaining omnibuses in Birmingham into the Birmingham & Midland Motor Omnibus Co Ltd, soon to abandon the motor omnibus in favour of horse omnibuses from 1907 until the motor vehicle had become more reliable in 1912.

The company tramways in Birmingham gradually disappeared as the leases expired between the years 1904 and 1911 due to the policy adopted by the corporation to take over and operate the tramways. The whole system was converted to overhead electric traction and a number of new routes were constructed.

ONE HUNDRED YEARS OF RAILWAY-ASSOCIATED OMNIBUS SERVICES

Charles E. Lee

Mr Lee is well known as a railway historian, but in this and the following paper he shows the depth of his knowledge of bus history. A founder-member of the Omnibus Society, Mr Lee is also one of its Vice Presidents, but it was as an ordinary member that he presented this paper to the Society in 1937.

In the two decades between the world wars, so much was written and said of the road versus rail war that the view has come to be accepted by many people that the two forms of transport are in essence, and always have been, opposed forces. Additional colour to this impression has been given by the fact that many people are aware of the existence, in 1835, of an Anti-Railroad Society under the management of Mr R. Cort. The *Anti-Railroad Journal*, which he ran, and similar literature of the same period, no doubt accurately represented a certain school of thought existing at that time, but it is entirely erroneous to suppose that anti-railroad views persisted widely, or even that they lived very long after 1835. In fact, friendliness and close working relationships between rail and road transport existed in Great Britain for practically a century.

At the outset, three points concerning the attitude of 1835 towards railways are worthy of mention:

1. During the last year of King William IV's reign the steam railway had established itself to the extent of being accepted as a practical means of transport. Money was plentiful in Great Britain, and investors were anxious to find a medium which promised a good return on their capital. Two more decades were to pass before the limited liability company as

we now know it, was introduced, and the investing public turned its attention therefore to the railway companies which, being statutory undertakings, offered a liability limited to the nominal value of the share and so avoided the perils of a holding in an unlimited partnership. The continued success of the Liverpool & Manchester Railway held out the promise of satisfactory dividends and so we find that during the Parliamentary session of 1836 no fewer than thirtyfive Acts of Parliament received the Royal Assent; twentynine were for new companies and authorised the construction of almost 1,000 miles of railways (955½ to be precise).

2. Nowadays we remember in the main only the surviving and successful railway schemes and are apt to overlook the fact that there were many wild-cat promotions which naturally were frowned upon by the responsible business men, and among them established road carriers.

3. Some of the leading supporters of the 1835 anti-railroad propaganda — such as Pickfords, Hornes and Chaplins — were astute enough very shortly afterwards to appreciate that the railway was destined to become the established trunk line means of transport, and to co-operate with, rather than oppose it.

The Liverpool & Manchester was the first railway in Great Britain to provide for both passenger and freight transport in the modern sense and we may therefore look to it for our first example of rail and road association. One of the earliest timetables (that dated February 1831) gives such an example, for it shows that the railway company provided connecting omnibuses at both ends of its line. At the Liverpool end the original terminus at Crown Street was outside the town and therefore buses were run on three routes from Dale Street to the station and were free to all passengers. In Manchester the old station in Liverpool Road was considerably more centrally placed so that although three bus services between the coach office in Market Street and the station were provided, and were also free, they were run only for passengers by the first-class trains. Before leaving this early timetable it is worthy of note that a list was appended of the coaches from Liverpool and Manchester to various parts of the kingdom.

Many examples might be quoted of other feeder bus services arranged by railways to serve outlying termini, but two will suffice. The first section of the London & Southampton Railway was opened for public passenger traffic from Nine Elms to Woking Common, on 21 May 1838. Facilities for reaching its London terminus were thus described by Arthur Freeling in *A Companion to the South Western Railway,* of 1840:

'The station at Vauxhall is 1 mile 77 chains from Charing Cross, and 3 miles 9 chains from the Royal Exchange. Omnibuses meet the trains from the City and the west end of the town; and, for the small charge of 4d the traveller may be conveyed there, by steam-packets which ply on the Thames, and start every half-hour from a wharf near London Bridge, calling at Waterloo Bridge, Westminster Bridge, Hungerford Market near the Strand, and several places on the Surrey side of the river; from these the passenger will be landed close to the station; he will then proceed to the booking office, take his place, and go through the office to the parade.'

Almost simultaneously with the LSWR was opened the first section of the GWR, namely Paddington to Maidenhead, on 4 June 1838. The company naturally desired reasonable access to its somewhat out of the way terminus and made arrangements with various bus proprietors to provide such facilities. The buses with which the GWR had relations were those of Sherman, Chaplin, Gilbert and Horne, which were specially put on to run between the GWR office in Princes Street at the Bank and Paddington station. The fare charged was originally a shilling a passenger, but because the traffic did not pay the GWR suggested a reduction to 6d a passenger on the principle that this would secure much better loadings and probably result in profitable operation. It was found in practice, however, that the bus proprietors incurred a considerable loss through this arrangement and in May 1839, they asked for and obtained a subsidy of 3d a passenger. These bus

RAIL—ROAD.

Interavailability of Tickets.

The return portions of Bus Tickets issued by Messrs. W. Alexander & Sons, Ltd., will be available by rail between corresponding Stations Aberdeen and Alford inclusive, while the return portions of Rail Ordinary, Tourist, Bulk Travel, Week-End and Daily Return Tickets (Cheap Holiday Tickets excepted), will be available by the Buses of Messrs. W. Alexander & Sons, Ltd., between the same points.

SEASON TICKETS.

Season Tickets are issued both by Railway and by Bus at reasonable rates.

For particulars of Rail Tickets apply to Stationmasters, or at Season Ticket Office, Joint Station, Aberdeen; and for information regarding Bus Tickets apply to the District Office, The Garage, Gairn Terrace, Aberdeen.

        Rail Phone - 3103.
        Bus Phones - 5056-7

Sc. T.S. 2634—(2,000).

JAMES BLAIR, 24 Market Street, Aberdeen.

London & North Eastern Railwa

AND

W. Alexander & Sons, Ltd.,

(Associated) Bus Service.

TRAIN and OMNIBUS

TIME TABLE

BETWEEN

Aberdeen, Kemnay,

Alford and Strathdon

STANCE – SCHOOLHILL.

24th AUGUST, 1932.

Until further notice.

(Fig 6) *(above and opposite)* Train and Omnibus Time Table, Aberdeen to Strathdon, from the Omnibus Society collection. The LNER bus services inherited from the Great North of Scotland company were later transferred to Alexanders, and this leaflet shows how the road-rail link was maintained

proprietors also carried parcels for the GWR in addition to passengers, as the railway offices in Princes Street included a receiving depot for parcels and goods.

The London & Croydon Railway provided an example of rail and road connections; this time with through booking. A timetable dated 13 May 1842, states that passengers may be booked at Croydon and Sydenham to the Bank, travelling by railway to New Cross, and thence by bus. In the reverse direction through bookings might be made at a confectioner's shop in Lombard Street whence the bus started. The through fares from the Bank to Sydenham were 1s 3d first class, and

Waiting and Tea Rooms on Top Floor of Schoolhill Station Buildings.

Aberdeen to Kemnay, Alford and Strathdon

	MONDAY TO SATURDAY										SUNDAY			
	Train a.m.	Train a.m.	Bus a.m.	SO Train p.m.	Bus p.m.	Train p.m.	Train p.m.	Bus p.m.	Bus p.m.	WSO Bus p.m.	Bus noon	Bus p.m.	Bus p.m.	Bus p.m.
Aberdeen	7·3	10·5	10·0	1·25	3·0	4·0	5·45	6·0	7·30	9·30	12·0	2·30	4·30	8·30
Blackburn			10·25		3·25			6·25	7·55	9·55	12·25	2·55	4·55	8·55
Kemnay	8·7	10·41	10·45	2·8	3·45	4·47	6·37	6·45	8·15	10·15	12·45	3·15	5·15	9·15
Monymusk	8·13	10·47	10·56		3·56	4·58	6·43	6·56	8·26	10·26	12·56	3·26	5·26	9·26
Whitehouse	8·27	11·1	11·13		4·13	5·8	6·57	7·13	8·43	10·43	1·7	3·42	5·43	9·43
Alford	8·32	11·6	11·30		4·20	5·14	7·2	7·20	8·50	10·50	1·14	3·50	5·50	9·50
		Bus					Bus							
Montgarrie		11·35		4·25			7·25	8·55			1·19	3·55	5·55	9·55
Bridge of Alford		11·40		4·30			7·30	9·0			1·24	4·0	6·10	10·0
Mossat		11·55					7·45				1·48		6·25	
Kildrummy		12·11					8·1				1·55		6·41	
Glenkindie		12·24					8·14				2·8		6·54	
Strathdon		12·49					8·39				2·23		7·9	
Corgarff (Allargue)		1·19 A					9·9 A							

Bus leaves from Schoolhill Station, Aberdeen.
A Ceases after 30th September.   SO Sats. only.
WSO Weds. and Sats. only.

Strathdon, Alford and Kemnay to Aberdeen

	MONDAY TO SATURDAY												SUNDAY			
	Train a.m.	Bus a.m.	Train a.m	SO Train p.m	SX Train p.m.	SO Train p.m.	Bus p.m.	Train p.m.	Bus p.m.	Bus p.m.	Bus p.m.	WSO Bus p.m.	Bus a.m.	Bus p.m.	Bus p.m.	Bus p.m.
Corgarff (Allargue)							2·45 AS				9·45					
Strathdon		7·00					3·15						8·30		5·15	
Glenkindie		7·40					3·25						8·40		5·25	
Kildrummy		7·55					3·40						8·55		5·40	
Mossat		8·2					3·47						9·2		5·47	
Bridge of Alford		8·20					4·5		5·20	9·5			9·20	4·20	6·20	10·5
Montgarrie		8·25					4·10		5·25	9·10			9·25	4·25	6·25	10·10
		Bus	Train				Bus	Train								
Alford	7·0	8·30	8·48	12·30	1·45		4·15	5·40	5·30	9·15		11·0	9·30	4·30	6·30	10·15
Whitehouse	7·6	8·37	8·54	12·36	1·51		4·22	5·46	5·37	9·22		11·17	9·37	4·37	6·37	10·22
Monymusk	7·17	8·54	9·5	12·49	2·4		4·39	5·57	5·54	9·39		11·24	9·54	4·54	6·54	10·29
Kemnay	7·24	9·5	9·12	12·57	2·12	2·12	4·50	6·4	6·5	9·50		11·35	10·5	5·5	7·5	10·40
Blackburn		9·25					5·10		6·25	10·10		11·55	10·25	5·25	7·25	11·0
Aberdeen	8·26	9·45	9·44	1·43	3·4	3·4	5·30	6·58	6·45	10·30		12·15	10·45	5·45	7·45	11·20

A Ceases after 30th September.
SO Sats. only.   SX Sats. excepted.   WSO Weds. and Sats. only.
AS Starts from Strathdon after 30th September.

1s second class; and to Croydon 1s 6d first class, and 1s 3d second class.

All these may be regarded as local feeder services, but *John Bull* (a Sunday newspaper) for 9 September 1838, in announcing the impending opening throughout of the London & Birmingham Railway, said that arrangements had been made with the principal coach proprietors for the establishment of branch conveyances to and from the railway stations and the neighbouring towns, the midland and northern counties, and North Wales.

In Lancashire early evidence of rail and road co-operation is provided by a card dated 15 July 1839, issued by the Manchester & Leeds Railway, and advertising the rail service between Manchester and Littleborough. This card announced that 'the Highflyer, Defiance, Celerity, Duke of Leeds, Cornwallis, Perseverence, and Miller coaches await the arrival of trains at Littleborough, and proceed immediately forward.' It was further stated that 'Wharton's omnibuses convey and take up passengers to and from Oldham going by the trains,' and that Marriott and Haynes's buses performed similar services for Rochdale passengers. 'Bradshaw' of 1841 referred to the fact that Furbisher's omnibus then ran to and from Oldham to connect with trains at Mills Hill station.

Another type of rail and road co-ordination was the provision by road transport of missing links in uncompleted railways. A well-known example is that of the London & Birmingham Railway. The first section, from Euston to Boxmoor, had been opened on 20 July 1837, and by 9 April 1838, had been extended to Denbigh Hall. On the latter date the Birmingham-Rugby portion was also opened. The Kilsby tunnel remained unfinished, so, in order to offer through facilities, Chaplin and Horne provided coaches and horses, to convey passengers and parcels over the unfinished portion between Denbigh Hall and Rugby. This arrangement was in force only for a few months as the railway was completed throughout on 17 September 1838, but during this period a very distinguished traveller used the combined rail and road route, namely Marshal Soult, the French Ambassador, and his son, the Duke of Dalmatia. On 20 July 1838, the party left Euston at 4.20 am and covered the 47½ miles to Denbigh Hall by 5.55; only five minutes were spent in making the exchange from train to coach at the little wayside inn at Denbigh Hall, by the side of the railway bridge across the London-Holyhead road. Benjamin Worthy Horne, the great coaching proprietor, was in charge of the arrangements, and to him we are indebted for the schedule. Rugby was reached at 9.20 and here fifty minutes were spent on breakfast. The party arrived at Birmingham at 11.10, having covered the 113 miles in 6 hours travelling time; this was the shortest recorded time in which the journey between London and Birmingham had ever been made. Ordinarily the schedule allowed 8½ hours for the combined rail and road journey.

Similar arrangements were made by the LSWR for a road link between Basingstoke and Winchester from 10 June 1839, until the completion of the railway throughout, on 11 May 1840.

A very fascinating example of through booking by rail and coach was arranged in order to give through facilities between Edinburgh and London and a waybill and tickets used on this service have survived. The North British Railway between Edinburgh and Berwick was opened on 18 June 1846. Exactly two years previously a continuous line of railway communication between Newcastle upon Tyne (or rather Gateshead) and London had been completed, and therefore there was an intervening stretch through Northumberland to be covered by coach. Before the opening of the Newcastle & Berwick Railway from Tweedmouth to Newcastle on 1 July 1847, passengers booking by the NBR completed their journey by coach. (The mail coach service between Edinburgh and Newcastle ceased on 5 July 1847, after having run for sixty-one years; latterly its speeds had averaged ten miles an hour.) Even then road transport was not entirely eliminated, for through passengers had to be conveyed between Newcastle and Gateshead by bus. The High Level Bridge across the Tyne was opened in 1850.

Naturally these connecting links were only temporary arrangements but all over the country coach and rail connections became an established feature.

In an outline of the relations between rail and road, the railway-owned local buses in London are worthy of attention. When the first section of the Metropolitan Railway was opened on 10 January 1863, the railway ran under the greater part of the New Road, which until then had been one of the main London bus routes. (The New Road had been built from Paddington to Islington in 1756, but was renamed in sections a century later. The portion in St Pancras was called Euston Road, the western end Marylebone Road and the eastern Pentonville Road under an Order of 20 February 1857). The LGOC naturally felt the effect of the competition, but very soon a little-known working agreement was reached, and the LGOC for seventy years refrained from competing with the Metropolitan Railway throughout its length, and, although buses covered the Underground routes in sections, they did not parallel it with a through bus route.

The Metropolitan Railway was extended on 23 December 1865 from Farringdon Street to Moorgate, which remained its eastern terminus for practically ten years. Having completed its main east to west line the railway company considered the question of providing adequate road connections from its stations to central points in the west end, and organised a service of horse buses between Portland Road Station (now Great Portland Street) and Regent Circus (now Oxford Circus). This route was opened on 6 August 1866, and extended on 2 February 1874 to Piccadilly Circus, where a Metropolitan Railway booking office was maintained for many years. At first the buses had both first and second class compartments, and the larger vehicles were drawn by three horses. All were distinguished by a large red umbrella over the box seat.

In 1872 the Metropolitan Railway wanted a bus connection to Camden Town and on 2 August of that year opened a service to and from Gower Street with hired vehicles. Just over a year later (on 26 September 1873) railway buses replaced the hired vehicles. Then on 16 May 1874, an LGOC service between Gower Street and Camden Town was opened and through bookings were continued with this.

First class bus accommodation ceased to be provided on 28 August 1882, and Metropolitan Railway tickets ceased to be available on the buses on 20 June 1889. The routes were frequently changed according to the pressure of competition, and the rise in importance of different localities. Perhaps the best remembered of those services is that between Gower Street and Edgware Road via Oxford Street and Marble Arch, which continued under Metropolitan Railway auspices until 31 October 1900.

In later years the Metropolitan Railway found it more convenient to arrange for all its bus services to be provided by outside contractors, and an LCC Report dated May 1895, gives the following particulars of routes run for the Metropolitan Railway with the familiar red umbrella on top over the driver:

SERVICE	BUSES OWNED BY
Baker Street Station – Piccadilly Circus	Edward John Ragg
Gower Street – Edgware Road	Andrews' Star Omnibus Co Ltd*
Moorgate Street Station – London Bridge	Edward John Ragg
Portland Road Station – Piccadilly Circus	Samuel Crews

Similar arrangements were made by the District Railway, and the same report of May 1895, listed the following details of District Railway bus services, which were distinguished by the emblem of a star carried on top:

SERVICE	BUSES OWNED BY
Blackfriars Station – Liverpool Street	Railways & Metropolitan Omnibus Co Ltd
Charing Cross – Volunteer, Upper Baker Street	London Omnibus Carriage Co Ltd.

* Note – The founder of this business was Solomon Andrews

Probably very few people realise that a railway company was directly responsible for the establishment of service 11 in London at the City terminus it has now used for nearly a century, but the North London Railway timetable for August 1870, shows this to be the case. It records that arrangements had been made with LGOC to extend to Broad Street Station the bus service working between Walham Green and the Bank via Charing Cross and Ludgate Hill. The same time-table also shows connecting buses between Hackney Station and Clapton timed to meet the trains.

Many examples might be quoted of the assistance given to railways in emergency by bus and coach undertakings, but one deserving particular mention has the double interest of referring to the famous road firm of Thomas Tilling and also to the well-known Folkestone landslip. The *South London Press* of 20 January 1877, gave the story in the following words:

'It was scarcely to be expected that the landslips and floods occurring at Folkestone would affect Peckham, but this seems to have been the case. I learn that Mr Tilling, the extensive Jobmaster of South London, has entered into arrangements with South Eastern Railway Company to horse several four-horse coaches to run between Folke-stone and Dover. The first number of horses left Charing Cross at 6 am on Thursday and others left the same evening.'

In horse-transport days, various feeder road services had been provided by contractors, and in some cases the main-line railways paid a subsidy to them. In January 1903 the Great Western Railway, for example, was expending more than £1,000 per annum by way of subsidy in connection with thirteen coach and horse-bus services to and from stations on various parts of the system. With the introduction of motors, the company was able in some cases to use its own motors in substitution for horse services provided by private owners, and thus save the subsidy. Four were as follows:

Route	Date motor service began	Annual subsidy saved
Moretonhampstead and Chagford	9 April 1906	£33
Modbury and Yealmpton	2 May 1904	£135
Saltash and Callington	1 June 1904	£156
Newcastle Emlyn and Cardigan	7 July 1920	£235

RAILWAY COMPANIES' ROAD POWERS

At the period when motors were being introduced, the specific powers possessed by the railways to work road services were very limited. The Furness Railway Act of 1 August 1899, enabled that company to work horse coaches in connection with or in extension of its railway system; the former North Staffordshire Railway had, by Section 27 of its Act of 24 June 1904, power to work road vehicles by animal or other power for goods and passengers in connection with or in extension of its system; and the former London & North Western Railway had, by Section 16 of its Act of 16 August 1909, power to run buses to or from the railways, but had no road power for goods. To these limited powers the London Midland & Scottish Company succeeded.

The Great Western Railway had no specific powers, but on grouping succeeded to the road powers possessed by the Cambrian Railways and by the Alexandra (Newport and South Wales) Docks & Railway. The Cambrian powers, under an Act of 24 June 1904, were for the conveyance of passengers, luggage, and goods in connection with or in extension of the system, and under these powers the Great Western Railway after grouping ran nineteen road services. The Alexandra powers were similarly limited. In the Great Western timetables, however, numerous road services were advertised, which were run without special powers. Their legality had been questioned, but no one moved for an injunction to restrain them, because they had been found to be in the public interest.

The Southern Railway succeeded to the road powers granted by the London, Brighton & South Coast Railway Act of

4 August 1906, for the conveyance of passengers and goods by road, but limited to cases where the traffic had been or was to be conveyed over some portion of the railway.

The widest road powers were those possessed by three constituent companies now forming part of the London & North Eastern Railway, namely the Great Eastern Railway (with Act of 24 June 1904); the North Eastern Railway (with Act of 11 August 1905); and the Great North of Scotland Railway (which secured powers in 1906). These companies were thus enabled to run road vehicles for passengers and goods in connection with or in extension of their respective systems or otherwise, subject however, in the case of the North Eastern, to severe restrictions in certain urban districts.

Pioneer honours among the large railways as a motor bus operator must be given to the GWR. Curiously enough the very first buses used were taken over from the road associate of another railway. The story began with Sir George Newnes's narrow-gauge enterprise, the Lynton & Barnstaple Railway, and its efforts to provide easy communication between Lynton and Ilfracombe. At first, horse drawn coaches maintained a service between Ilfracombe and Blackmoor station on the narrow gauge railway, but early in 1903 Sir George Newnes, with characteristic enterprise, decided to work motors. He bought two 22-seat 16 hp Milnes-Daimler motor wagonettes and formed a company which inaugurated the service in June of that year. A contemporary London newspaper comment said, 'This is the first time that a railway has started a motor-car service to collect and distribute passenger traffic, and it may be hoped that the example thus set may be followed by some of the great companies.'

By a curious coincidence the example was not only quickly followed by the GWR, but the first enterprise of the latter was actually begun with the same vehicles, for the Lynton & Barnstaple Railway found its enterprise unpopular in a district where horse-drawn coaches were at the height of their popularity and, following difficulties with the police as to 'speeding above 8 mph' disposed of the two Milnes-Daimlers to the

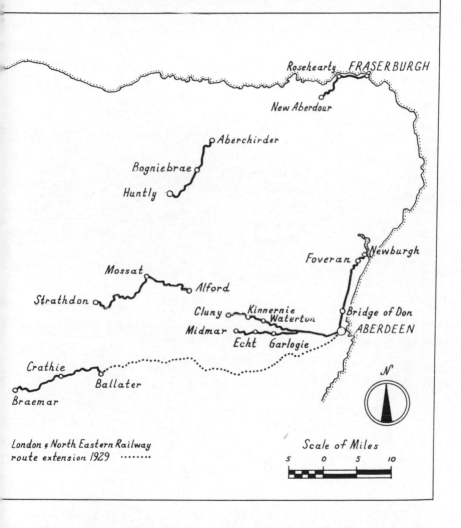

GREAT NORTH OF SCOTLAND RAILWAY
MOTOR BUS SERVICES - 1912.

(Fig 7) Map of GNSR services. Drawn by E. Axten after data in British Rail Archives

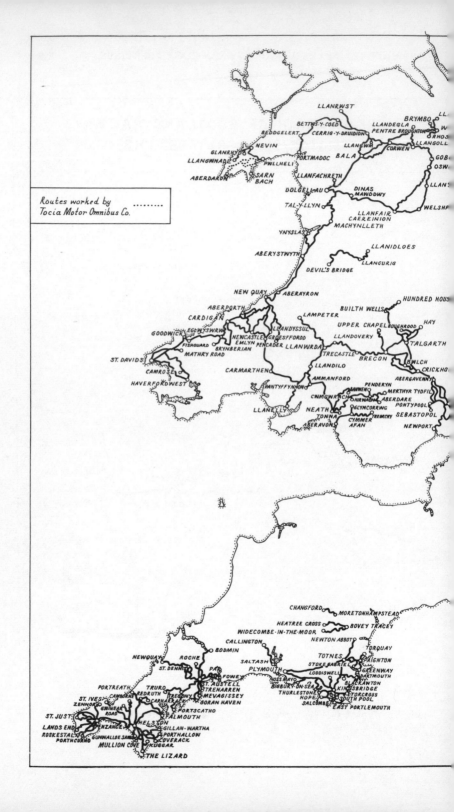

Routes worked by
Tocia Motor Omnibus Co. ....

GREAT WESTERN RAILWAY MOTOR OMNIBUS ROUTES 1929

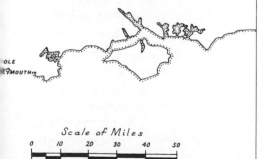

(Fig 8) Map of GWR services. Drawn by E. Axten after data in GWR Memorandum by Mr F.J.C. Pole dated December 1926, and other sources

GWR. It was with these that the latter inaugurated its famous Helston to the Lizard route on 17 August 1903. The reason for opening a service in this remote part of Cornwall was that local interests were requesting a light railway to be built and the GWR was unwilling to incur the expense (estimated at £85,000) without first testing the traffic potentialities of the route. Subsequently other services were used in this way, and in at least one case revealed sufficient traffic to justify building a railway, but in many other instances hundreds of thousands of pounds on light railway constructions were saved. The following tables gives a few examples:

Route and estimated cost of Light Railway		*Remarks*
Helston and The Lizard	£85,000	GWR motor service began 17 August 1903
Calne and Marlborough	£75,000	GWR motor service began 10 October 1904, but failed to pay and was suspended 30 September 1913
Windsor and Ascot	£424,849	GWR motor service began 5 April 1905
Penzance, St Just and Land's End	£140,000	GWR motor services began: Penzance to Land's End, 3 April 1904; Penzance to St Just, 16 May 1904
Saltash and Callington	£120,000	GWR motor service began 1 June 1904, replacing subsidised horse service

Many amusing incidents might be told of those pioneer days. For example, on the first trip from Helston to the Lizard with a Mayor and other guests, the bus made such slow progress that a costermonger in a donkey cart headed the procession and beckoned the motor driver to come on.

The Lizard service was suspended for a short time, from October 1904 to April 1905, in consequence of a dispute with the local authority about damage to the roads. It is not without interest to recall that this service, and others started a little later by the GWR, were nearly abandoned owing to the high cost and unreliability of tyres; the cost worked out at about 3d a mile.

Incidentally, this service, together with others established up to late in 1904, was run contrary to legal requirements. The Locomotives on Highways Act of 1896 applied only to vehicles under three tons in weight, and, as manufacturers could not produce public service vehicles to comply with this requirement, advantage was taken of the fact that no regulations were in existence showing what should or should not be included in the weight of the vehicle. The obstacle was overcome by removing items of equipment from the cars and painting the chassis 2 tons 19 cwt. The regulations were modified in 1904 to the extent of permitting the use of motor vehicles up to five tons in weight without a pilot.

Although the pioneer service did not prove a paying proposition in its early stages, results were sufficiently promising to justify the commencement of another route, and that between Penzance, Newlyn, and Marazion (three miles) was opened on 31 October 1903. The results of these two services led to the placing of an order for thirty Milnes-Daimler vehicles in 1904.

Thereafter, many services were opened in various parts of the railway company's area, and for thirty years the Great Western Railway Company played an increasingly important part in the provision of motor bus services throughout the territory covered by its railway system, and although such services were always operated as feeders to the trains, the term feeder was interpreted very widely, probably more so than with any other British railway company.

The first GWR bus service in Devon was that between Modbury and Yealmpton (twelve miles) begun on 2 May 1904.

Sir Tristram Eve and a local company (the South Hams Motor Carriers Ltd) also ran a car on the route, and both this and the GWR bus often failed — sometimes at the same time. The railway company eventually took over the locally-owned service, and the transaction is of interest as being probably the first railway *acquisition* of a motor service. Another very well-known and old-established GWR route in the neighbour-hood of Plymouth was that between Saltash and Callington (9½ miles) which began on 1 June 1904.

For a variety of reasons some of the early GWR bus services were discontinued and between 1903 and 1909 no fewer than seventeen services were tried and given up because the traffic offering proved insufficient to support them. However, the fleet of buses grew steadily. It reached thirtyfour on 31 December 1904; fiftysix on 30 June 1905; seventytwo on 31 December 1905; and eighty on 31 December 1906. The early choice of Milnes-Daimlers proved as satisfactory to the GWR as it did to the Vanguard company in London and out of the total of eighty, above mentioned, no fewer than sixtyseven were of this make. By June 1907, GWR buses had run up-wards of 1,600,000 miles and carried more than 3,500,000 passengers. In January 1908, the GWR bought fourteen Milnes-Daimler double-deck buses from the Associated Omni-bus Co Ltd of London and its fleet then totalled about 106 Milnes-Daimlers, with seven of other makes. By 1911 some thirtyone GWR services were working.

The first world war necessarily resulted in the suspension of some services, but in 1919 the GWR was working 110 buses over thirtythree routes, the length varying from three miles between Uxbridge and Denham (a service begun on 11 Jan-uary 1917, and worked with double-deck buses) to twenty-one miles between Abergavenny and Brecon. A war-time expedient to keep buses working during the period of acute petrol shortage was the use of coal-gas containers, an experi-ment begun in December 1917.

After the war, the GWR showed very considerable enter-prise in opening new services, as well as restoring those that had been suspended as a war measure. Many of these came under the heading of general development, and were justified on commercial grounds. There were also some which were regarded as necessary for traffic development, but were not in themselves financially profitable; and in a few cases routes were opened on grounds of policy. An example of the last-named was the service between Reading, Sonning and Twyford, which was established on 2 October 1924 as a substitute for a rail halt near Sonning, the estimated cost of which was £7,500.

As this post-war development was parallel to the rapid spread of provincial motorbus companies, the statutory authority of the GWR to act as a motor bus operator was queried by rival interests. The present writer attended a meeting of substantial provincial bus proprietors as early as the summer of 1921, when this matter was discussed, but no one moved for an injunction to restrain the GWR, and thus test the legality of its operations, because the company's road services had been found to be in the public interest.

Early in 1925, however, the company's rights to develop its bus services were questioned through the medium of the London and Provincial Omnibus Owners' Association, in respect of operations in the West of England and in North Wales. As a result, agreements were reached with the Devon Motor Transport Company, the Cornwall Motor Transport Company, and the Crosville Motor Company. These agreements were of value in avoiding wasteful competition, as they clearly allocated existing routes to one or other of the parties, on an agreed basis. The agreement with the Cornwall Motor Transport Company became effective on 1 May 1925, when certain GWR activities were discontinued under the reciprocal arrangements. These agreements were not one-sided, for the Crosville Motor Company handed over to the GWR such services as Brecon-Talgarth-Hay (on 13 July 1925), and Corwen-Llandrillo (on 1 October 1925).

About this time negotiations took place also, but without any immediate material result, with the Devon General

Omnibus & Touring Company, the Bristol Tramways & Carriage Company and the Birmingham & Midland Motor Omnibus Company. In the London area a *modus vivendi* had long since been reached with the London General Omnibus Company. One of the early GWR road services, that between Slough and Windsor (begun on 18 July 1904, to supplement the rail service), had been discontinued by arrangement with the LGOC on 28 July 1913, and the LGOC had given an undertaking not to compete on weekdays with the GWR service to Farnham Common.

During 1925 no fewer than eighty small, fast buses were added to the GWR fleet and many new services were inaugurated. At the end of that year the company had 206 buses which produced a gross revenue of £152,000, against 118 vehicles and £49,695 revenue of the other three railway groups combined. GWR expenses, however, exceeded revenue by £3,361.

The accusations sometimes levied against our railway companies that they were unwilling to co-operate with other undertakings is certainly not exemplified by the story of the GWR road motor department, and in South Wales in particular numerous arrangements were made between the railway company and various bus proprietors that were entirely independent of railway shareholders. To quote but one example, reference may be made to the non-competitive agreement arrived at in March 1927, between the GWR and James & Sons, of Ammanford, which provided not only for the establishment of joint schedules but also for inter-availability of return tickets. Incidentally, it was during 1927 that the GWR was approaching its peak of bus operations, and in that year the directors authorised the purchase of seventyfive 32-seat buses. Over eight million passengers were carried in the one year and more than 4,800,000 miles were run.

In January 1928, the GWR took over the Dare Valley Motor Company of Aberdare, and in September of the same year F.T. Rosser's Motor Services working in East Monmouthshire. By this time the GWR was working no fewer than 168 services and had 300 buses on the road.

The four main line railway companies secured their comprehensive road transport Acts on 3 August 1928, and this marked the beginning of the end so far as direct railway operation of buses was concerned. The strong legal position then possessed by the railways enabled them to make arrangements with the large provincial bus companies. It is worthy of note that the GWR road activities in Cornwall and Devon were of sufficient size and importance to justify an amalgamation, and not merely a railway purchase of shares in a bus company. In January 1929 the Western National Omnibus Co Ltd was formed to amalgamate the GWR services in the west of England, and those of the National Omnibus & Transport Co Ltd. Thereafter, similar arrangements were effected throughout the GWR area, and by the end of 1931, details had been concluded for the transfer of all GWR bus services to road operators. Actually, the Slough-Beaconsfield route passed to London General Country Services Ltd, on 10 April 1932, and the Slough-Taplow route to the Thames Valley Traction Co Ltd, on the same date. These were the final transfers with the exception of the joint GW & SR services at Weymouth.

Obviously it is impossible to dwell in detail on such a widespread organisation, but four services of special interest are deserving of mention. The first is the Slough-Beaconsfield route, which was begun on 1 March 1904, and is thus the oldest motor bus route of London Transport. Then there is the Wolverhampton-Bridgnorth service, a route of about 15½ miles, which was also opened in 1904 – on 7 November to be precise – and was turned over to Wolverhampton Corporation on 1 July 1923. An Oxford-Cheltenham coach service opened on 29 October 1928, in connection with a joint rail and road schedule between London and Cheltenham. The road section was taken over by the Bristol Tramways & Carriage Company Ltd on 8 February 1932. The Weymouth-Wyke Regis service, the last to work in GWR livery, was originally begun on 26 June 1905, but was suspended from 31 August 1909. It was resumed on 22 July 1912, as a joint GWR and LSWR enterprise (but maintained by the GWR), and as such was taken over by the Southern National Omnibus Company Ltd on 1 January 1934. This closed the GWR direct operation of bus services.

As already mentioned, the Cambrian Railways were authorised by Act of 14 June 1904, to run motor cars. In June 1906, the company inaugurated a Pwllheli-Nevin service with two Orion 2-cylinder single-deck buses seating twentytwo passengers; two with driver, eight in an open smoking compartment, and twelve in the main body. The Cambrian interest was purchased by Nevin Omnibus Company, which took over the service on 14 February 1913, and continued to run the buses in co-operation with the railway. The business was incorporated as the Nevin & District Motor Omnibus Co Ltd on 15 March 1913, and continued to maintain the service until it was taken over by the GWR in September 1925. At one time Parliamentary powers were sought for a Pwllheli-Nevin-Abersoch railway in Lleyn peninsula but the plans were deferred.

We now turn to the London Midland & Scottish Railway group, which included chiefly the old London & North Western Railway and the Midland Railway in England, and the Caledonian, Glasgow & South Western, and Highland railways in Scotland. Space will not permit us to deal in detail with more than one of the many LMSR constituents, and the obvious choice must be in favour of the LNWR.

Although the Great Western Railway is entitled to pioneer honours as an operator of motor buses, the LNWR had a far longer record of bus working, for its horse services ran on many feeder routes in the last quarter of the nineteenth century.

One of these old established LNWR routes was that between Boxmoor Station and Hemel Hempstead. This service was begun with horse buses in April 1884, and continued as such for over twentyfive years, until in August 1909, single-deck Milnes-Daimler motor buses were substituted, providing accommodation for twentyfive passengers and also mails and parcels. In 1912 single-deck Leyland vehicles were introduced on the service and continued working throughout the war period. They were replaced in 1922 by Thornycroft chassis with bodies built at the railway carriage works at Wolverton. Normally, one bus sufficed for maintaining the service, which consisted of about twentyfour double trips in connection with trains, a double crew covering about seventeen hours daily in traffic. In March 1928, a second bus was put into regular service and a number of additional trips scheduled. In February 1929, the bus service was amplified and certain journeys were extended to work through between Boxmoor and Harpenden, a distance of ten miles, largely in replacement of passenger trains on the Midland section Harpenden-Hemel Hempstead branch. The branch was never a busy one for passenger traffic, but Hemel Hempstead needed some direct facilities to and from the Midland main line, and many of Dickinson's employees at Apsley Paper Mills were carried morning and evening. For their convenience a halt was opened at Heath Park, and certain trains were extended there from Hemel Hempstead. Various attempts had been made to develop passenger traffic, which explains why there were no fewer than three halts between Harpenden and Hemel Hempstead, besides the one intermediate station at Redbourn. The situation was, however, compromised by running a limited passenger train service, for which the engine otherwise engaged in branch goods traffic was used, and other facilities were given by the Boxmoor-Harpenden bus service. Three additional buses were placed in service for the extra traffic, and including provision for special workmen's trips to and from Dickinson's works, the fleet at Boxmoor then consisted of six Leyland Lion and one Albion 32-seater single-decker observation coaches (one vehicle spare). The bodies of the Leylands were built at Derby, LMSR. Provision was made for reasonable luggage and the buses continued to carry mails, newspapers, etc, as in earlier days. Garage accommodation was provided in the goods yards at Boxmoor station, where there was room for three buses in the old horse stables.

One of the little railway-controlled horse bus services which eventually grew into quite a large business was that between Watford Junction station and the town. At the Olympia Motor Exhibition in November 1905, considerable interest was taken in a double-deck bus on the Milnes-Daimler stand finished in the well known livery of the LNWR with the company's coat of arms instead of a fleet name on the side panels. On 23 April following (1906) this bus went into service between Watford Junction Station and Croxley Green and not only replaced the old town horse bus but also provided Croxley for the first time with a regular transport service. The popularity which attended the venture resulted in a new service being inaugurated on 30 July 1906, between Watford and Harrow stations via Bushey. It will be recalled that until 10 February 1913, there was no through railway from London serving the station at Watford High Street, and electric traction followed only in 1917. The LNWR buses in question were not at first licensed in the Metropolitan Police Area, as on every journey they went beyond its limits. However, in August 1907, five LNWR Milnes-Daimlers were licensed by Scotland Yard notwithstanding the fact that they still generally went outside the Metropolitan Police Area on each journey. By 1914 LNWR bus operations in the Watford area had reached quite considerable dimensions, but in July of that year the Watford-Harrow service, which for some while past had formed the most important of the Watford group of the LNWR – five Daimlers and four Leylands had been employed on it – was given up. This was in consequence of the starting of a new LGOC service between Watford, Bushey Heath, Stanmore and South Harrow, and thereafter the railway buses worked from and to Watford night and morning only, in order to maintain the LNWR service from Harrow to the top of the Hill and to Pinner. After the war the LGOC covered much of the Watford territory in lieu of the railway company. A service between Golders Green and Boxmoor was opened on Good Friday, 2 April 1920; Croxley Green-Garston; and Bushey-Boxmoor, both daily, in September 1920; and Bushey-Hemel Hempstead in October, 1920. The service from Golders Green was withdrawn at the end of the summer season, but the remaining routes were transferred on 1 June 1921, to the National Omnibus & Transport Co Ltd which worked them as operating agent on behalf of the LGOC under an agreement dated 21 July 1921. In common with similar National-worked services to the north of London, these passed to London General Country Services Ltd on 1 March 1932, and came under the ownership of the London Passenger Transport Board on 1 July 1933. Thus the present group of bus routes in the Watford neighbourhood can claim lineal descent from the horse enterprise of the old LNWR.

One more isolated LNWR service in the London area was that between Tring station and town which was started in 1914. This never developed into more than a link between railway and town, excepting that on Fridays and Saturdays a few trips were run to Aldbury, about a mile from Tring station, for market and shopping traffic. The vehicle latterly used by the railway company was a 1928 Leyland 32-seater on Lion chassis, which went to Tring in September 1929, after working for a time at Rochdale. It was garaged in a wooden shed in the goods yard at Tring station and was worked by two drivers and two conductors, who also cleaned the vehicle. These buses were painted in LMS lake colour below the waist line.

Although so far we have dealt with the routes of the old LNWR in the London area, this was not the first district the railway served with motorbuses. As long ago as 10 July 1905, the familiar and handsome chocolate-and-white livery of the North Western Railway appeared on a motor bus when the company opened the Connah's Quay to Mold route with a double-deck 34-seat Milnes-Daimler, with a Mercedes engine, very similar to the well-known 'Vanguards' in London. This was followed on 11 October 1905, by the famous Holywell station and town service, over which eighteen journeys a day were maintained on a route with a gradient as steep as 1 in 9. The services in North Wales were subsequently developed considerably and in 1914, when war broke out, quite a network of routes was in existence there. Impressment of buses for war purposes resulted in suspension of activities, and the railway services were never resumed.

In the summer of 1914 the LNWR passenger motor fleet totalled forty, and its composition was as follows:

CENTRE		VEHICLES
Watford	1	double-deck Commercar
	6	double-deck and observation Daimler
	13	double-deck and observation Leyland
Tring	1	observation Commercar
Brownhills	1	double-deck Commercar
	2	double-deck Milnes-Daimler
Mold	5	double-deck and observation Commercar
Holyhead	2	observation Commercar
Llandudno Junction	9	double-deck and observation Commercar

Total 40

The Midland Railway was never an extensive motorbus operator but, nevertheless, that company worked one or two interesting services. In London, it established an inter-station motor bus between St Pancras and Victoria, via Charing Cross, with a single-deck Thornycroft vehicle, as early as July 1905. (Both the Great Northern Railway and the London & North Western Railway had been interested in similar horse-drawn services, maintained by contractors, but all such activities were discontinued from 1 October 1913).

Apart from those in Northern Ireland (which are outside our scope), the other Midland services were designed mainly to serve Rothwell, in Northamptonshire. To that point a service was opened from Desborough station in May 1908, the Midland Railway Company's own buses (a Maudslay and a Wolseley) replacing those previously worked by a private contractor. The Desborough-Rothwell route was discontinued in July 1911, and the Midland Railway then served Rothwell by buses from Kettering.

An early example of a bus to the rescue when a railway failed was given when the narrow-gauge section from Waterhouse to Hulme End was duly opened on 27 June 1904, but, owing to earthwork slips, the standard-gauge link from Waterhouses to the main railway at Leek was not available. A steam bus was put on to span the gap, and, despite breaking down on the inaugural journey, successfully maintained the service until 1 July 1905, when the railway was in order.

The LNER group included three railways that entered the field of motor bus operation in very early days. Taking them in order of seniority in this sphere of activity, we come first to the old North Eastern Railway.

When the North Eastern Railway placed its first motor bus on the road, on 7 September 1903, between Beverley and Beeford, it was only three weeks behind the GWR. There is no doubt that the GWR was the first, but that company suspended operations for a short time and thus broke the continuity of its working, whereas the NER ran buses without a break on the Beverley-Brandesburton route and thus in past years challenged the GWR claim.

In October 1922, a private competitive service was run, but failed and was discontinued; to be followed in May 1923, by another of the Newington Motor & Engineering Co Ltd. On 1 October 1925, the LNER bus service was abandoned and continued by the Newington company. It was arranged that the company should bring its buses into Beverley station yard and connect with the trains. The Newington company passed into the hands of the East Yorkshire Motor Services Ltd in May 1932. The North Eastern Railway also developed numerous bus services in County Durham, and these were eventually taken over by United Automobile Services Ltd on 1 January 1930.

The Great Eastern Railway decided in 1903 to run buses and selected Lowestoft to Southwold as its first route. Its officials were sent down to Cornwall to watch the GWR experiment, and as a result road powers were immediately sought. These were granted by the Company's Act of 24 June 1904, and immediately the Lowestoft-Southwold service was begun. It continued under railway ownership until January 1913, when it was turned over to the United Automobile Services Ltd. That company agreed to work the route in co-ordination with the train services and the railway company thus secured the road link and at the same time avoided competition with the road company.

Far more interesting of the GER activities were those around Chelmsford, for they formed the nucleus of the present Eastern National business. On Saturday, 9 September 1905, the GER began a series of services radiating from Chelmsford to Danbury, Great Baddow, Writtle, Broomfield, and Great and Little Waltham. The Chelmsford branch was turned over to the old National Steam Car Co Ltd, on 21 July 1913. A point of interest that is unusual is that the GER built for these services in its locomotive works at Stratford the first motor buses ever constructed in the works of one of our great railways. The chassis was notable for its robust construction even at a time when weight reduction did not receive much attention. Another feature was the braking equipment, for besides the usual shaft and wheel drum brakes, slipper brakes acted on the tyres and a sprag was fitted. These buses had 38 hp engines. Twelve in all were built and were used in various parts of East Anglia including the famous Ipswich-Shotley service which survived the war period and was finally purchased by the Eastern Counties Road Car Co Ltd in April 1922.

The Dee-side area provided an extensive field for services of the Great North of Scotland Railway, the first of which began on 2 May 1904, and extended for nearly seventeen miles between Ballater and Bracmar. Here the motorbus experienced two difficulties peculiar to the neighbourhood. One was the local preference for the old four-in-hand stage coach, and the other the rigours of the climate. The former was overcome by

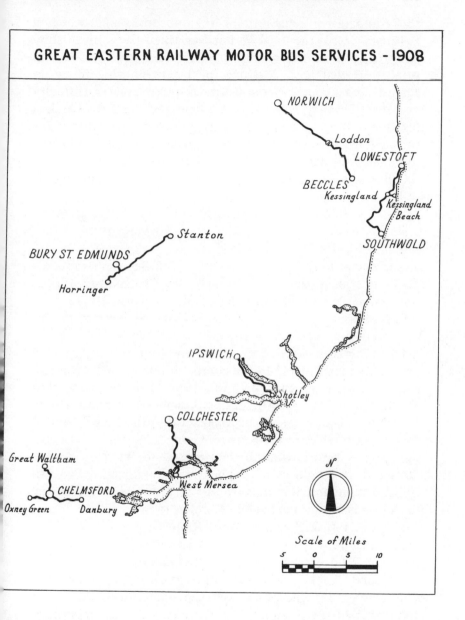

(Fig 9) Map of GER services. Drawn by E. Axten after data in British Rail Archives

the comparative reliability of the motorbus and when in February 1910, the local authorities asked the railway company to suspend the service in order to spare the soft and thinly metalled road, a strong local petition was drawn up against such a course. Snow storms proved a greater difficulty and in 1908 they were so severe that the road was blocked for some time. When eventually a bus from Ballater got through the driver received a great welcome at Braemar and someone even wrote a poem in his honour.

Other services in the neighbourhood were inaugurated as follows:

ROUTE	MILEAGE	DATE BEGAN
Huntly-Aberchirder	11¾	1 May, 1905
Alford-Strathdon	19½	1 May, 1906
Aberdeen-Cluny	16½	1 September, 1906
Aberdeen-Midmar	17	1 November, 1906
Aberdeen-Newburgh	15¼	1 April, 1907
Fraserburgh-New Aberdour	9½	18 November, 1912

These services survived grouping and were even extended under the LNER. In 1929 the company introduced a through route between Braemar and Aberdeen via Ballater and thus duplicated the Ballater-Aberdeen rail facilities. Interavailability of tickets was introduced. In August 1930, the LNER handed over these services to the Scottish General Northern Omnibus Company Limited, whence they passed to W. Alexander & Sons Ltd. It should be mentioned however that the Scottish General company was already in the group, control having been purchased by the SMT in March 1930.

The London & South Western Railway was never a large motor bus user, but one or two of its ventures deserve brief mention. The earliest was a nineteen-mile service between Exeter and Chagford which was opened on 1 June 1904, with a Milnes-Daimler. The service was suspended during the winter and resumed on 3 June 1905 with two 32 hp single-deck Clarkson steamers. These were succeeded by Thornycroft petrol buses and the service continued to be railway-operated until some years after the first world war.

A different type of experiment was that on the Farnham to Haslemere route. Here a contract was made with John L. Thornycroft & Co Ltd to maintain the route for one year under an agreement whereby the railway took the receipts and guaranteed 10d a vehicle mile to the contractors. The service was begun in February 1905, with one bus and at the end of the twelve months receipts exceeded the guaranteed 10d a mile by about £115. The railway company thereupon bought the bus and continued to maintain the service until 1913 when it was handed over to the Aldershot & District Traction Co Ltd.

On 11 December 1905 the Mersey Railway began a motor bus service between Birkenhead Central Station and the residential district of Oxton, and the activities were extended on 29 January 1906. In all, ten double-deck buses on Saurer chassis were bought. The service was withdrawn on 8 March 1906 as the result of an injunction granted at the instance of Birkenhead Corporation, as the Mersey Railway had no specific powers to operate road services. The Court of Appeal later said that the railway company might carry bus passengers, but only to or from its stations. On this basis, the buses began working between Rock Ferry Station and the Lever soap works at Port Sunlight on 16 May 1907, but bus operations were finally abandoned on 8 July 1907 as a result of a House of Lords Judgment.

After the granting of general road powers to the four main-line railways on 3 August 1928, the LMSR and the LNER each began buying shares in various bus companies which were independent of the Tilling and British Electric Traction Groups. Outstanding was the old Crosville Motor Co Ltd, which was purchased outright by the LMSR in October 1929. Later that year, arrangements were made by the railway companies with both Groups for co-ordinated working of rail and road services, and the relative railways acquired in most of the operating companies in England and Wales a shareholding interest equal to that held either severally or jointly by the Tilling and BET Groups. Comparable arrangements in Scotland were made between the LMSR and LNER and the Scottish Motor Traction Co Ltd.

This position remained substantially unchanged until railway nationalisation at the beginning of 1948, with the railway companies owning shares equal to the other large shareholder in many provincial bus companies. On 1 January 1948 such railway shareholdings were vested in the British Transport Commission. In September 1948 the latter purchased the shareholdings of Thomas Tilling Ltd in provincial bus companies, and so became the owner of many of the companies. These interests passed to the Transport Holding Company on 1 January 1963. Then, in March 1968 the BET sold to the Transport Holding Company all its holdings in the seventeen provincial bus companies in which it shared control with the THC, and also in seven other companies heretofore without nationally-owned shareholdings. The THC thus became the controlling factor (and in many cases the outright owner) of the large provincial bus companies, only to be succeeded on 1 January 1969 by the National Bus Company in England and Wales, and the Scottish Transport Group north of the Border.

RAILWAY COMPANIES IN THE BRITISH ISLES THAT HAVE OPERATED MOTOR BUS SERVICES DIRECTLY OR BY CONTRACT

Compiled from Mr Lee's paper; from *The Rise and Decline of the Railway Bus* (J.M. Cummings: Paper presented to the Omnibus Society, 1957); and from other sources. Dates in *italic* are doubtful, and further information on the subject will be welcomed by the Editor.

RAILWAY COMPANY (CNT indicates services provided by contract	LOCATION OF SERVICES	DATES OF OPERATION
Alexandra (Newport & South Wales) Docks and Railway	Newport Mon.	1906-*1924*
Belfast & Northern Counties Railway	N Ireland	1902-1904
Belfast & County Down Railway	N Ireland	1916-*1935*
Bishops Castle Railway	Shropshire	1928-*1932*
Caledonian Railway	Glasgow	1905-*1908*
Cambrian Railways	Nevin, N Wales	1906-1913
Campbeltown & Machrihanish Railway	Kintyre	1931-?
Corris Railway	Mid Wales	1908-1930
County Donegal Railways Joint Committee	Donegal	? - present
Glasgow & South Western Railway	SW Scotland	1906-?
Great Central Railway	SE Lancs	1905-1906
Great Eastern Railway *(some CNT)*	E Anglia &c	1904-1922
Great Northern Railway *(CNT)*	London	1914-?
Great Northern Railway (Ireland)	Ireland	1929-1958
Great North of Scotland Railway	NE Scotland	1904-1923
Great Southern & Western Railway (Ireland) *(some CNT)*	Ireland	1910-?
Great Southern Railways (Ireland)	Ireland	*1934*-1944
Great Western Railway	Various	1903-1934
Guernsey Railway	Guernsey	1909-present
Isle of Man Railway	Isle of Man	1928-1930
Jersey Eastern Railway	Jersey	1926-1929
Jersey Railways and Tramways	Jersey	1923-1931
Lancashire & Yorkshire Railway	SW Lancs	1907-*1909*
London Midland & Scottish Railway	Various	1923-1933(1)
London & North Eastern Railway	Various	1923-1930(1)
London & North Western Railway	Various	1905-1923
London & South Western Railway *(some CNT)*	Various	1904-1923
Londonderry & Lough Swilly Railway	Donegal	1929-present
Manx Electric Railway	Isle of Man	1907-?
Mersey Railway	Wirral	1905-1906 & 1907
Metropolitan Railway	Watford	1927-1929
Midland Railway *(some CNT)*	Northants	1908-*1921*
Midland Railway (Northern Counties Committee)	N Ireland	1904-*1935*(2)
Midland & Great Western Railway	Ireland	1911-1916 1924-?
North British Railway	E Lothian	1905-?

North Eastern Railway	Various	1903-1923
North Staffordshire Railway	N Staffs	1904-1905
Portpatrick & Wigtownshire Joint Railway	Galloway	1907-1908
Sligo, Leitrim & Northern Counties Railway	Ireland	?-?
South Eastern & Chatham Railway *(CNT)*	Hythe, Kent	1914
Southern Railway *(some CNT)*	Various	1923-1934

NOTES — (1) The LNER and LMSR continued to be interested in bus operation until 1947, through membership of Joint Committees with Halifax, Huddersfield, Sheffield and Todmorden corporations.   (2) In these cases, operation was not continuous throughout the period.

Contract Services are those provided by road operators but for which the railway concerned undertook full financial responsibility. In certain other cases (not recorded here) railway companies provided a subsidy for a service or group of services.

The state transport undertakings (British Transport Commission, Coras Iompair Eireann and Ulster Transport Authority) have been omitted from this list as having a generalised tunction rather than being examples of railway undertakings running motor buses.

A CHAPTER IN LONDON BUS HISTORY

Charles E. Lee

Symbolic of Mr Lee's place in the study of transport history is the inclusion of two of his papers in this collection. This personal sketch of one of the pioneers of the industry was issued by the Omnibus Society after the war as a special paper.

The death on 4 April 1948 at Bournemouth of Colonel Frank Searle, CBE, DSO, passed almost unnoticed, particularly in the motor press, and this is the more surprising in view of the prominent part he took in connection with the London bus industry during the important period immediately before the 1914 war. As the first really successful chief engineer of the London General Omnibus Co Ltd, and the one responsible for the company designing and building its own chassis, he has a claim to be remembered, apart from his less-known activities in relation to the inner politics of the industry.

After a locomotive engineering training, he turned to road transport, and was among those early motorbus engineers who established themselves as consultants; his office was at 1, Upper James Street, Regent Street, W. He went to Paris in 1905 and became responsible for importing two types of French bus chassis, namely, the Tyrgan and the Lacoste-Battman. His first connection with the London motorbus industry that is known to me was in September 1905, when he acted as consultant to Balls Brothers, the then well-known horse bus proprietors of Brixton, in connection with the purchase of a Tyrgan motorbus. Then he arranged to sell Lacoste-Battman chassis to the London & District Motorbus Co Ltd (the 'Arrow' fleet), which was one of the Salisbury-Jones group of companies, of which the best known was the

Vanguard. As these vehicles were not entirely satisfactory for London bus service, the major portion of the order was cancelled, and Searle gave up his own business to take a staff job with the Arrow buses.

He then applied for the position of superintendent of Mortlake Garage, London General Omnibus Co Ltd, and was interviewed by the board of directors on more than one occasion. Eventually, on 14 February 1907, he was appointed at a salary of £350 per annum, subject to one month's notice on either side. The manager of the company's motor department at that time was John Henry Fooks-Bale, primarily an electrical engineer, and formerly engineer and tramways manager to Walthamstow Urban District Council, who had found the task of managing the miscellaneous LGOC bus fleet somewhat beyond his capacity. Within three months, Searle was transferred from Mortlake (which was used exclusively by De Dions) to the chief depot at Dollis Hill (Cricklewood), where no fewer than twentyeight types of motor vehicles shared the premises with a stud of some 300 horses. In May 1907, Fooks-Bale resigned to take up another appointment, and Searle was one of the five candidates on the short list for succession. At a board meeting on 16 May 1907, Searle was appointed chief motor engineer of the LGOC at a salary of £450 (increased to £500 on 1 January 1908) which included the charge of the motorbus fleet of 145 working vehicles and also his remaining responsible as manager for Dollis Hill Garage. Thus began the eventful period of serious changeover from horse to sound mechanical transport, for which Searle was mainly responsible, and which was undoubtedly the salvation of the LGOC. Searle was a staunch and able advocate of steam propulsion, and it was his strong advocacy at the time of his appointment as chief that saved for further experiment the Clarkson steamers, after the decision had been taken to withdraw them owing to very high cost of upkeep. He then designed in May 1908, a bus combining the recognised lightness and strength of the De Dion chassis with the Clarkson steam engine, and the prototype was ready in August. It consisted of one of the LGOC De Dions converted by Thomas Clarkson at Chelmsford. Meanwhile, the first great London motorbus amalgamation had taken place as from 1 July 1908, comprising the LGOC, the London Road Car Co Ltd, and the Vanguard Motorbus Co Ltd. Searle survived the amalgamation as chief engineer of the greatly-enlarged undertaking, to which the LGOC contributed about 300 motorbuses to a combined fleet which Frank Pick stated in 1928 to have totalled 994. This total is probably about 100 in excess of the vehicles actually in service. The fleets at work on 1 July 1908 would appear to be: Vanguard 380; LGOC 267; and London Road Car 237; making a grand total of 884.

Shortly after the amalgamation the directors were contemplating a further order for about 200 Wolseley buses, when Searle suggested that the company should design and manufacture to its own particular requirements. It already possessed overhaul works at Walthamstow, inherited from the Vanguard Motorbus Co Ltd, and here the original X type was completed on 12 August 1909. It was licensed on 16 December and sixtyone in all were built. Experience with the X type resulted in the production of the famous B type, of which the first was completed at Walthamstow on 7 October 1910, and licensed on 18 October. These chassis, tested and ready for the body, cost well under £300 each, and were a main feature of the rehabilitation and success of the LGOC. In fact, such was this success that early in 1911 there were rumours of various schemes for new London bus companies backed by powerful financial interests. One of these was the Premier Motorbus Co Ltd, backed by the Daimler and BSA group. Searle was approached to become its general manager, but refused to commit himself until the company was formed. Doubtless it offered financial attractions, as, despite his outstanding success, his salary with the LGOC was then only £1,000 a year, and the appointment was subject to a quarter's notice. At the beginning of May, Searle's name was being mentioned publicly in connection with the proposed new company, and he was interviewed by the LGOC board of directors on 4 May

1911. He was offered a 5-year agreement a year, subject to immediate acceptance, and, on his declining to commit himself without time for consideration, it was resolved that his appointment with the company be terminated. The secretary was instructed to pay him three months' salary in lieu of notice. Searle then accepted the position of general manager of the new company, which was about to issue its prospectus. At the same board meeting, Walter James Iden was appointed chief engineer of the company under agreement for a period of five years at a commencing salary of £1,000 per annum, rising by annual increments of £100, but the directors retained the option of dispensing with his services at any time during this period on payment of one year's salary. In fact, he remained as chief engineer until 1917.

At the eventful board meeting of the LGOC, one further important step was taken, which was destined to stifle the new bus company, but to understand the significance of this it is necessary to go back a few years. An earlier effort had been made by the Daimler interests to enter the London bus field, when their chairman (Edward Manville) headed the Gearless Motor Omnibus Co Ltd, which was incorporated on 31 March 1906, and reconstructed on 23 May 1906, with exclusive rights to use the petrol-electric system of Henri Pieper of Liége in London bus service. The authorised capital was £220,000, of which £215,000 was in £1 ordinary shares and £5,000 in 100,000 deferred shares of 1s. A prospectus of 24 May 1906, offered the ordinary shares for subscription; £50,000 was underwritten, and this was stated to have been subscribed by 27 August 1906, but the issue was clearly not successful. A contract was entered into with the Daimler Motor Co (1904) Ltd for the supply of ten buses (against the 150 gearless and twentyfive ordinary which the prospectus contemplated); The Daimler Co was to run the ten at its own risk for twelve months, paying the Gearless Co one half the net profits. Because of altered police regulations, the type of bus had to be redesigned entirely, and only trial runs took place. The company lay dormant with only £26,050 of its ordinary capital and all the deferred shares actually allotted and called up. In 1910 the Daimler group produced the KPL bus, also a petrol-electric, under the patents of Knight, Pieper and Lanchester. This was worked experimentally in Birmingham, and was to be the vehicle used by the Premier Motorbus Co in London.

In 1907 a petrol-electric bus had been devised for the use of Thomas Tilling Ltd, as that company was experiencing difficulty in training its horse staff to manipulate the clutch and gear box. This vehicle was made under the patents of the SB&S Syndicate, of which the initial letters indicated the names of the joint inventors — Percy Frost-Smith, Engineer & Manager of Tilling's motor department, Frank Brown, Chairman of David Brown & Sons Ltd, of Huddersfield, and W.A. Stevens, Managing Director of W.A. Stevens Ltd, of Maidstone. The chassis of the original vehicle was built by J. & E. Hall Ltd of Dartford, and included that company's 30 hp engine. It began work in January 1908. An improved form of this vehicle was afterwards marketed under the name Hallford-Stevens.

This was the background at the time of the LGOC board meeting on 4 May 1911, which Richard S. Tilling attended with Walter Wolsey jr and explained that Frost-Smith and two others had a patent petrol electric transmission; that Thomas Tilling Ltd had an option to buy it for £3,000; that the Daimler Company's KPL bus infringed this; and that the Daimler Company had offered to purchase the rights from the patentees for £5,000. Richard Tilling suggested that it might be to the interest of the LGOC to purchase the patent. It was resolved that the question be referred to the Solicitors for advice and that the General Purposes Committee have power to act in the matter.

At the LGOC board meeting on 11 May 1911, the directors at the request of Richard Tilling took into consideration the action of Thomas Tilling Ltd in bringing this matter to their notice, and it was resolved that in consideration of Thomas Tilling Ltd securing all rights under Patent Nos 7054/07 and

4976/09 and assigning them to the London General Omnibus Co Ltd that day for £3,000, together with the right of directing at the expense of the company, but in the names of the patentees, any litigation in connection therewith that the company might desire and such litigation being successful in preventing the new company from coming into operation, it was agreed that, should the LGOC propose to establish a motor route upon any of the roads then worked by Thomas Tilling Ltd, a proportionate number of motors should be worked on such roads from end to end in a ratio of 1 to 3, provided that the number of working motorbuses in the hands of Thomas Tilling Ltd should not at any time exceed 150.

The patent objection was found to be valid, and Frost-Smith lodged an objection before the Comptroller of Patents on behalf of the SB&S Syndicate. The principal ground of objection was the method of driving by twin independent worm gears through independent electric motors outside the frame on each side of the chassis, securing by electrical means the effect of a differential. The flotation of the Premier Motorbus Co was postponed, and, as events proved, abandoned. Incidentally, the company of similar title which was formed in January 1912, and introduced some De Dion buses in London in September 1913, was an entirely separate enterprise.

There had been a sharing arrangement between Tilling and the LGOC since 6 May 1909, in respect of all motorbuses, but this new agreement established the figure of 150 for the first time as the Tilling share of the London bus business – it was substantially larger than the Tilling motorbus fleet at that time. A comprehensive agreement between the parties was made on 15 May 1912, and replaced by a modified agreement (for twenty years) on 6 October 1913. Thus began the recognition that Tilling should own a 5 per cent interest in the London Bus Pool.

Frank Searle joined the Daimler Company at Coventry to inaugurate a commercial vehicle department, and once again he came into conflict with the LGOC. A highly efficient bus was evolved, using the 40 hp Daimler (Knight) sleeve-valve engine. This was offered at £825 complete with 34-seat body, tyres, and electric lighting set. Searle approached the British Electric Traction Company for an order on behalf of its Metropolitan Electric Tramways, working in the northern part of London which were fearing intensive competition from the LGOC. The original memorandum of association of that company had empowered working only up to fifteen miles from the GPO, and at the time the Underground Group took over control in January 1912, it was announced officially that 'the company will extend its London services within approximately a fifteen-mile radius.' Very shortly afterwards, however, the company's plans envisaged serving a greater area, and the thirty-mile radius from Charing Cross was adopted. The Metropolitan Electric Tramways formed an associated company called the Tramways (MET) Omnibus Co Ltd on 13 January 1912, to work motor buses in connection with the tramways, at the time when the BET Group was embarking extensively on motorbus operation in the provinces. Searle booked an initial order from the BET for the first 100 Daimler buses, and undertook a maintenance contract for a period of three years for labour, material, petrol and lubrication at a charge of 3½d a mile. He afterwards approached Albert Stanley (later Lord Ashfield) and asked him if he would like to purchase Daimler buses, telling him that the Daimler Company had sold 100 vehicles for use in connection with the Metropolitan Electric Tramways. Stanley suggested giving an order for 250 buses, if the Daimler Company would undertake not to supply motorbuses to any other London operator for a period of five years. This information was duly conveyed to the BET, which increased its order to 350 buses; at the same time the maintenance contract was reduced from 3½d to 3d a mile. The British Automobile Traction Co Ltd (a BET subsidiary) placed an order for ten Daimlers for London service in May 1912; this was afterwards increased to thirtythree. The first went into service on 7 October of the same year on the Victoria to Liverpool Street route, and rumour had it that the fleet was to be increased by six a week for some time ahead. There is some uncertainty about the precise size of these orders, particularly in connection with the MET, as the BET Group was ordering many Daimlers at this period for its associated companies. In August 1912, the MET order was widely publicised by the Daimler Co as 300 chassis, 'the largest bus order ever placed,' but the fleet supplied was 350.

At this time the Underground Group decided to segregate its motor manufacturing activities from the LGOC, and the Associated Equipment Co Ltd was incorporated as a private company on 13 June 1912, to take over the business and the Walthamstow works, which had been established in 1906. Shortly afterwards the LGOC itself was reconstructed and the new LGOC was incorporated on 25 July 1912, to take over the assets and liabilities and undertaking of the 1858 company. A non-competitive agreement was reached with the British Electric Traction Group regarding London area business, and the London & Suburban Traction Co Ltd was incorporated on 20 November 1913, to acquire controlling interests in the Metropolitan Electric Tramway Ltd (95 per cent), the London United Tramways Ltd (97 per cent) the Tramways (MET) Omnibus Co Ltd (100 per cent), and other companies. In May 1913, the South Metropolitan Electric Tramways & Lighting Co Ltd (nearly 100 per cent), was added to the list. The combined activities of these companies included 123 miles of tramways and light railways, several important electricity supply undertakings, and about 380 motorbuses. All but the London United Tramways had been in the BET Group; the LUT was contributed by the Underground Group. In December 1912, an agreement was concluded between the LGOC and the BET Group defining the area outside which the LGOC agreed not to operate, and arranging a working agreement for all traction business within the London area. For many years, both Groups had large shareholdings in the London & Suburban Traction Co, but in November 1928 the BET disposed of its interest to the

Underground Electric Railways Co of London Ltd.

In consequence, when the first of the new MET fleet of Daimlers appeared on streets on 28 January 1913, the buses were worked under agreement by the LGOC; the whole fleet of 350 vehicles was in operation by August 1913. A parallel thirty-year working arrangement with the British Automobile Traction Co Ltd was made on 22 January 1913, but the 'British' buses were not worked by the LGOC, although they came into the London Traffic Pool. At the annual meeting of the Gearless Motor Omnibus Co Ltd a few days later, the Chairman, Edward Manville (of the Daimler Company) announced that an agreement had been entered into with the LGOC under which the Gearless Company would be entitled to run twenty buses in London for a period of at least thirty years. There were incidental agreements with the London & Suburban Traction Co Ltd and with the Daimler Co Ltd. These twenty Daimler buses were placed in service on 5 April 1913, and were worked by the LGOC. (Thus, the only buses which the company owned were not 'gearless'). The London & Suburban Traction Co acquired 12,977 ordinary (out of 100,000) shares in the Gearless Company in January 1913, but Edward Manville retained his directorship until the undertaking of the Gearless Company was taken over by the LGOC on 1 January 1922. A fleet of ten B-type buses was placed in service, under the fleet name 'Southern', by the LGOC on 1 August 1913, on behalf of the South Metropolitan Company.

The LGOC did not wish to assume the maintenance contract with the Daimler Company, so the latter was compensated for loss of profits and also was appointed sole selling agent in November 1912, for any surplus vehicles made at Walthamstow. The working arrangement between the Daimler Co and the Associated Equipment Co provided for buses and some sizes of commercial vehicles to be made at Walthamstow. Because of inadequate production facilities for commercial vehicles at Coventry at that time, the AEC constructed chassis at Walthamstow and equipped them with Daimler engines from December 1913, until the 1914 war. By reason of these arrangements, which were in operation during the early days of that war, all vehicles made at Walthamstow for the War Office were sent out from there as Daimler products, but with distinctive type letters to differentiate between the Walthamstow and Coventry vehicles. The chassis of the original 350 MET buses, after two years of service, were repurchased by the Daimler Co and sold to War Office as reconditioned vehicles. After the 1914 war the AEC and Daimler companies developed their own separate businesses, and their subsequent relationships (such as their two years of combined production under the Associated Daimler Co Ltd from 1926) are beyond the scope of the present notes.

Although Col Searle went to Munich in connection with the inauguration of a Daimler bus service by British interests, and subsequently visited other parts of the world on behalf of the Daimler Company, his association with the London bus industry was finished. During the 1914 war he served with distinction in the Tank Corps, and was awarded the DSO in 1918 and the CBE in 1919. After that war he was connected with car hire and aviation* on behalf of the BSA-Daimler Group.

* In 1926 he became the first managing director of Imperial Airways. For an impression of his impact upon commercial aviation see John Pudney: *The Seven Skies* (Putnam, 1959), especially p.58 (Ed)

EXTENDED TOURS BY MOTOR COACH

E. L. Taylor

Mr Taylor was President of the Omnibus Society when he read this address in 1963. His career has been largely with companies in the British Electric Traction group, but in addition he has taken a prominent part in the affairs of the British Travel and Holidays Association.

May I first of all tell you of the pleasure it gives me to become your President. The Omnibus Society is a unique institution; I know of nothing else quite like it. Its extensive and peculiar activities have been known to me, in varying degrees of intimacy at irregular intervals, ever since I was first pulled into the passenger road transport industry – as it were, through a side door – in the year 1920. My respect and regard for your Society, for its enthusiasm and its sheer erudition, has mounted with the years. So your invitation was immensely flattering and pleasing, but in relation to my duty this evening, rather frightening. I studied the addresses of my distinguished predecessors, and wondered how I could find something to talk about that had not already been adequately dealt with.

Then your immediate past Chairman put into my head the idea that I might deal with the touring side of the industry, which does not seem to have been done before – so if this was a poor idea, he must take some share of the blame.

Now, you are called the Omnibus Society, and I started with some slight hestitation on account of that name. Most, if not all of you like to be regarded as busmen – I do myself – and at least in my younger days there was a tendency in some quarters to regard a bus and a coach as two different animals. We were very busy indeed in those days, building up bus services in particular, under considerable pressure and in conditions which, until the 1930s, often approached the chaotic, so that it was perhaps not surprising that some staunch busmen were inclined to regard coach operations with suspicion as an irritating diversion of effort. What one learns in youth is hard to forget. In the end I convinced myself that if the Chairman of the Omnibus Society could himself suggest a dissertation on touring coaches, then this possibly junior relation must really be accepted as a respectable member of the honourable family.

In any case, the common ancestry of the coach and the omnibus becomes clear enough in terms of history. All through the records, mankind has displayed the habit of banding together for the adventure of travel, with a wide variety of objectives. I suppose that the Canterbury Pilgrims, the Crusaders and the mercenaries, who wandered over Europe in the middle ages, used individual transport, on foot or on horseback, but the citizens of Athens who made up their chariotloads for Corinth and Epidaurus, the gay cavalcades to Bath or Tunbridge Wells, the expeditions of the Pickwick Club and suchlike were identifiably passenger road transport. Sometimes they were omnibus traffic and sometimes they were a private party on a special occasion, and apart from outward appearances they undoubtedly had a lot in common with the crowds at Victoria coach station any day in the year.

For the first three thousand years or so of developing civilisation the natural and inevitable line of inland communication was the road. Then, in the first half of the nineteenth century the evolution of the steel rail – seventy years before the rubber tyre – brought about a great change in the pattern of things. The railways rapidly took over all serious travel and expanded it enormously, stage coach services were discontinued, the roads fell into neglect, and some actually disappeared altogether. Even in this period of eclipse, however, a small lamp was kept alight. The 'pleasures of the road' is no empty phrase, and against all odds a large volume of short distance pleasure traffic was carried in horse brakes and wagonettes.

The word 'charabanc' was imported to describe a horse-drawn passenger vehicle with transverse bench seats, and it was when this was at last motorised that the open road started to come back into its own.

The first motor omnibuses — or coaches, for it would have been hard to distinguish them then — came in with the turn of the century. One need not be an old man to remember them. Chancy vehicles of uncertain temper and impolite habits, churning up dust, belching smoke and sometimes steam, not very comfortable, they yet appealed to the tough in body and adventurous in spirit, of whom there were plenty. They caught on, and thus encouraged they improved quite rapidly, as I am sure the archives of your Society will display. Their first function, long before anyone thought of using them for a regular service, was to succeed and replace the horse-drawn charabanc on day and half-day trips, and in the terms of my earlier remarks, this, so to speak, is where we came in. Many of the older-fashioned proprietors, horse-lovers to a man, bitterly resented the rising newcomers, and when ridicule failed to defeat them there were many fierce battles in council chambers and on sea-fronts. But the tide had gathered strength in favour of the motor, and by 1905 or so hardy spirits were banding together for daring sorties in these juggernauts, and a new era had begun.

The brave men who took their courage in both hands and invested their money in the new and temperamental monsters were content for some years to keep them near home, and welcomed each safe return with a sigh of relief. But before very long the urge to expand the horizon got the better of them and the first extended tours began.

Authentic data is hard to find. I tried about ten years ago to assemble some early facts, and I obtained the most valuable assistance from Mr Charles E. Lee. I imagine the annals of the Society contain a variety of interesting references. It seems certain, however, that the firm of Chapman's of Eastbourne (taken over by Southdown in 1932) advertised and operated a six-day tour of North Wales in 1910, with a 22-seater Dennis vehicle, and this may well have been the pioneer of all that has followed. In the next two or three years they expanded the programme far and wide – even to a twentyone day tour to John o' Groats. From the north, Standerwick's of Blackpool in 1912 operated an eight-day tour to London and the South Coast in a Karrier open charabanc. It was driven by the late Mr E.V. Standerwick, who died on 31 October 1962. The journey to London took two days with an overnight stop in Lincoln, and spare cans of petrol were carried on the steps. In 1913 those dauntless pioneers, Messrs A.E. Cannon and A.D. Mackenzie were in charge of Worthing Motor Services, which was an original constituent on the formation of Southdown two years later. They exploited the holiday tour market vigorously under the name of 'Sussex Tourist Coaches', and in that year their programme – using both Dennis and CC-type Daimlers – included both the Lake District and a 'Seven Counties in Seven Days' tour to the south-west that took in both Porlock and Countisbury hills. Their 1914 brochure features the Daimler 'Silent Knight' coach, and refers to – '... the cover over the top, which together with the glass windows all round enables the passengers to take advantage of all weathers ... whilst perfect ventilation is ensured in the clerestory ventilators.'

Strange to think that a problem we still worry about was evidently solved fortynine years ago. Maybe we should have another look at the clerestory ventilators.

The same brochure also expresses the hope – 'that the ladies will wear hats or caps as small as possible. It is very unfair to other passengers if their view is obstructed by the hats or feathers of ladies in front of them.'

I am old enough for that to conjure up a sweet nostalgic memory-picture.

The fares were curious in two ways, a tour for which a single passenger paid 5½ guineas could be had by two seated side-by-side for ten guineas, and the seats in the front row cost 10s each extra.

Development came to an abrupt halt with the outbreak of

war in 1914; but one military operation can be said to have blazed a new trail, for the 'Old Bill' type London buses which carried so many thousands of troops up to the front line were almost certainly the first such vehicles to cross the Channel to Europe.

As soon as that war was over, many enterprising operators set about re-establishing the holiday tour market. Chapman's were again in the fore-front, and in 1919 or 1920 they ran six-day tours of the battlefields of France and Flanders. These were very probably the first Continental tours by British coaches; the solid-tyred Dennis 20-seaters they used were subsequently converted to pneumatic tyres. By 1921 they had reached the French Riviera, followed in the next two or three years by tours to Holland, Germany, Italy and Spain – this last took 22 days and visited Gibraltar. But they were not alone. About the same time, the late Mr W.P. Allen, in charge of London and South Coast Motor Services (later taken over by East Kent) also ran short tours from Folkestone and other towns in Kent to Belgium, Holland and the battlefields. The vehicles were transhipped by cargo steamer and for some years they had offices and garages at Ostend and Blankenberg.

Meanwhile, some remarkable pioneering work was also accomplished by Motorways of London, which was then in charge of Messrs Graham Lyon and H.J. Spencer.* These enterprising young men realised that the postwar demand for seats in the Blue Train, and indeed all services to the South of France, far exceeded the supply, so they acquired from the American army in France two trucks, a White and a Chevrolet. On these they installed French coach bodies equipped with sunshine roof, twelve or fourteen swivelling armchair seats, a buffet-kitchen and a toilet compartment,

---

* Graham Lyon left Motorways quite early, and after a varied career became a hotel proprietor, and subsequently pioneered the motel. He died on 21 April 1963, leaving Watney Lyon Motels as a memorial. H.J. Spencer eventually became Motor Transport Superintendent for the British Overseas Airways Corporation; he died on 10 April 1966.

and in 1920 these two vehicles inaugurated a regular service from Calais to the Mediterranean. In the next two years they added a Berliet, two Saurers and (in 1922) the three Dennis coaches which were the first British vehicles in the Motorways fleet, and these last were transhipped across the Channel. Pneumatic tyres had been fitted by this time, and the touring range extended over most of Europe. Indeed, the original White and Chevrolet penetrated North Africa in 1924, but a later thrust towards Istanbul was defeated by bad roads and got no further than Belgrade. But you may be interested to know that the same firm ran a tour to Leningrad and Moscow in 1935.

The twenty years between the wars saw an immense improvement in the motor-coach itself – in speed, reliability and comfort. In the mid-nineteen-thirties I must have travelled some thousands of miles in such vehicles as the Leyland Tiger and the AEC Regal, the latter with fluid transmission and both with petrol engines. The timber-built bodies we used were not so tough as the metal construction of today and had a shorter life, but they were the product of fine craftsmanship, and as road surfacing and the pneumatic tyre also improved enormously they gave a riding quality comparable with the best we can achieve now. Or so it seems from memory; certainly it compared very well with the private car of the same period. By about 1934 we had a motor-coach we could with all confidence send off wherever there was a road to take it and count on its return to the hour and minute of the timetable. Between 1920 and 1939 (despite the economic setback of 1930/1) the climate was favourable for expansion of the coach holiday market in other ways. There was a large increase in the grant of holidays with pay throughout industry and it is probable that the total number of people taking annual holidays away from home multiplied by three or four times. The ownership of private cars increased rapidly, and this had its part in breaking down the long-established practice, among a large section of the population, of taking a static annual holiday. Touring holidays, mainly by road, increased enormously and hotels and caterers had to meet the changing trend. Some were reluctant, but many wayside inns realised that a new potential offered itself and did very well out of it.

By and large, the bus and coach industry was not slow to exploit the trend. There were, as I said in opening, some curious exceptions among busmen − those with a preoccupation with stage carriage service and a suspicion of coach operation − and to this day there are companies of a fair size which have never run extended tours. But where that was the case others stepped in, and by or before 1939 coach tours in quantity were on offer from every large centre of population and many small ones too. Until about 1935 most of us were busy enough making the most of the attractions of our own country, of which there is no shortage, but if we were to hold our market we must offer variety and we started to look overseas for it. Thenceforward British coaches became an increasingly familiar sight on the main roads of Europe. The tourist-conscious governments encouraged the traffic, and obstacles were few and far between. The pound sterling was strong and continental costs comparatively cheap. Even the mounting political tension of the late 1930s had very little impact on coach tourists, who were apt on return to wonder what all the fuss was about. Germany in particular erected a façade which was more than the holiday visitor (except accidentally and very rarely) could penetrate − aided, of course, by the natural friendliness of ordinary people. After Munich the atmosphere changed, and the tourist demand in that direction steeply declined.

The declaration of war in September 1939 was followed by some months of suspended animation that I imagine few of us who can remember would care to live through again. Fuel was rationed but government policy favoured maintaining an atmosphere of normality, and we were actually encouraged to continue a restricted programme of recreational traffic. Some few holiday tours were operated until June 1940, by which time all the signposts had been taken down. It took

the Dunkerque evacuation and its aftermath to bring us face
to face with reality; after that we had other things to do and
think about for six years or so. Many of our coaches were
pressed into military service — I seem to remember the RAF
impressment officers were always keen to take the best they
could find.

When the war in Europe came to an end, we did succeed in
getting some of them back again. Word would come from
various sources — usually, but not always military — that a
fleet of vehicles assembled somewhere might contain some of
ours, and we would then go and examine them. They had all
lost their civilian registration plates on impressment, of course,
and we had to seek engine and chassis numbers — a laborious
business much simplified in the case of my own company at
that time by a curious circumstance. Before the war we had
employed in most garages a portable electric engine starter of
our own design, which required a square spigot to be welded
on the forward end of the starting handle shaft, and this
provided a ready means of identification, visible from twenty
yards. Some of these coaches were in surprisingly good condition, having been well maintained and less hard worked
than those we had been left with, and we were glad to have
them.

Getting coaches in motion again on extended tours in a
world of rationing and chronic shortages was a formidable
task. Many hotels that had been taken over for military and
other warlike purposes took a long time to release and still
longer to recondition. Controls of all kinds, as always, took
far longer to relax than to impose. At the same time the
demand from a war-weary public was tremendous, and when
in 1946, after great efforts and against some tricky hazards, we
managed to put out some sort of programme, all the seats we
could offer were sold out in a few days. I do not think anyone
succeeded in transhipping a coach to the Continent in that
year. In 1947 there was a small improvement in this country,
and some expansion in operation, and we did succeed, by
curious means, in shipping a coach across to Calais, by way

of a freight train ferry, which was the continuance of an operation instituted in the latter part of the war. It had to be a small one — on a Bedford petrol-engine chassis — and it had to stay in France for the whole season, but with the blessing of the French authorities it accomplished a season of fourteen-day 'circular tours' to the Riviera with great success — to everybody's slight surprise. In fact, the official French attitude was far more welcoming and benign than it has become in these sophisticated days; we had more difficulty in persuading the Bank of England to let us have the francs we needed for operating costs. At that time, tourists going into Europe could claim a foreign currency allowance of £75 plus the return railway fare. I well remember a long argument in Threadneedle Street early in 1947 based on the calculations that twentyeight passengers to Nice, and return by train would involve a total sterling outlay of about £480, whereas we could perform the same operation by motor coach for a quarter of that sum. And when at last we had convinced our masters on this point, we had to start all over again with a campaign in favour of the genuine necessity of the journey two of us must make, in order to complete the detailed accommodation arrangements. We succeeded with about thirtysix hours to spare.

In 1948 it again became possible to tranship coaches by crane via Dover/Boulogne, and to a small extent via Dover/Ostend, whilst the Dover/Dunkerque train ferry also came back into service. During 1951 loading ramps were constructed at both Calais and Ostend; and in 1952 also at Boulogne, so that the similar double-ramp construction at Dover in 1953 established the drive-on and drive-off system which has worked so well ever since. Indeed, it is difficult to imagine how the traffic volume could otherwise have been handled, because the 360 transits in 1948 increased year by year and the total has been around 3,000 since 1958.

The international regulations governing the operation of motor-coaches across the frontiers of Europe which have broadly and generally allowed freedom of movement to a vehicle passing in and out of each country with the same complement of passengers (defined as a 'closed-door' tour) were consolidated in a Convention on Road Traffic signed at Geneva in 1949 and since ratified by most European governments. This has become known as the 'Freedom of the Road' agreement, and although some countries have tended to apply their own definition of the word 'freedom' it has generally worked satisfactorily. Indeed, some governments have made concessions, such as to permit foreign coaches to remain in the country between tours on defined conditions and in appropriate circumstances, in order to encourage the valuable tourist traffic. Incidentally, this agreement does not apply between our own mainland and any part of Ireland, but in recent years both Irish governments, North and South, have conceded entry permits for coaches across the Irish Sea. In 1954 a new and more comprehensive outline agreement was established under the auspices of the Economic Commission for Europe. Basically, it is founded on the existing regime; details are to be incorporated in a formidable series of annexes, and on these, argument has so far gone on for eight years. Some progress has been made, but since the objective is to cover every aspect of international transport by road it is not really surprising that it should take a long time to formulate regulations acceptable to all the widely varying views of the participants. In the meantime, some continental governments have sought to impose regulations of their own which we would certainly regard as restrictive, and whilst these have little effect at present on the operation of British coaches abroad, they hold a certain danger for the future.*

* The debate within the European Economic Community, which had gone on for eight years prior to the preparation of this paper in 1963, still continues. Some countries, notably Belguim, Italy and Spain, still insist on a lot of documentation, but this appears to be due to bureaucracy rather than anything else. The exception is France, where in my experience there has always been a powerful faction which would rather retain one single passenger for SNCF than admit a thousand by any other means. As a result of restrictionist regulations, British operators take ingenious routes to minimise the use of French roads.

For the three years prior to 1963 we were thankfully free of currency restrictions for travel abroad, but in the first ten post-war seasons there were wide fluctuations which created difficult problems. In October 1945 the annual allowance started at £100; in March 1946 it was cut to £75, in August 1947 to £35 and in the following month it was abolished altogether. In April 1948 it was re-introduced at £35 and then swung to and fro between £50 and £100 until 1952, when it was cut again to £25. This last was a cause of alarm and dismay, but as things turned out it served to display how cheaply a week's holiday abroad could be organised. Of necessity, shorter tours were operated at lower fares than ever before, with the result that the total market was expanded rather than otherwise. The allowance was raised to £40 in the following year and increased by stages until it was, for all practical purposes, relaxed altogether — but there is no doubt in my mind that the 1952 restriction gave birth to the ultra-cheap continental holiday which has been something of a mixed blessing ever since.

Another revolution in modes of operation in recent years has followed the vast increase in air travel. The first air-coach tours in substantial volume commenced in 1954 with a short cross-Channel hop instead of the much longer transit by sea. Deeper penetration by airplane journey followed quickly, with Luxembourg as a popular 'port of entry.' In 1963 flights of five or six hundred miles to join the coach will be by no means uncommon, and there is no indication that the limit has been reached. How far it will be found economic to send out a British coach on these terms, and how far the definition of a 'closed door' tour can be expanded, are questions yet to be resolved, but the trend will undoubtedly continue.

I seem to have spent a lot of time on the particular aspect of coach tours overseas. With all the expansion that has occurred, however, the major volume of traffic on extended tours has always operated within our own frontiers and I suppose it always will. The operational problems involved are common also in varying degrees to those encountered on the continent of Europe; in varying degrees, because Great Britain was, by comparison with the greater part of the continent, a latecomer to the tourist market, and — again by comparison — poorly supplied with suitable hotels. In my own early days, many hotels in this country, were strongly prejudiced against coach touring parties; they seemed to think they might wear improbable clothes and comic hats, and blow tin trumpets. I can remember my surprise, in the mid-nineteen-thirties, by the welcome we got at such renowned hotels as the Waldlust at Freudenstadt or the Richemond at Geneva. There were some very good hotels in this country with a friendlier attitude, but they were in a minority and they were often managed by people who had some continental experience. Times have changed under the pressure of holiday trends and economic circumstances, but a lingering hostility is still to be found here and there in unexpected places.

As well as good coaches and good hotels, successful operation demands good organisation, staff and publicity. Inside the office, the devising of each tour for every hour of its programme calls for the most painstaking attention to detail. Careful timing is of the essence of the matter. The passenger wants to make the most of every precious minute of his holiday, but without being hurried, which can be an interesting exercise in reconciling the irreconcilable. Each season some will return and say that it was all very enjoyable but we tried to cover too much in the time available, so will we please put on a new tour with fewer stops and more time at each point of attraction. This we try to do, and then discover once again what a high proportion of the public, having studied the whole programme, decides that the best value for money is the tour which appears to cover the widest area in the period available. On the other hand, there has also been a growing demand in recent years for tours concentrating on one or two main centres — at the expense of long journeys outward and return.

The selection and training of road staff is a vitally important matter; obviously the skill and ability of the driver and courier will make or mar the success of any tour. It is an interesting and attractive job, very satisfying for the right type of enthusiast and reasonably rewarding. But enthusiasm is not enough. Properly done, it is very hard work, and apart from a thorough knowledge of all the attractions of the tour and the ability to pass it on entertainingly to thirty or forty people, it calls for a fund of tact and patience. The majority of holiday-makers are kindly, considerate and appreciative, but the occasional crosspatch can upset a whole party and may need very careful handling indeed. I suppose I make the good courier sound a complete paragon; and there are never enough paragons to go round. Very occasionally we have the time to sit and think about all the things that – with all our care – could go wrong but do not.

Publicity is a vast subject on which whole papers have been written. In the case of extended tours, the essential basis is the annual brochure, and a close study of the hundreds of glamorous productions issued each December might well leave the impression that in some cases, almost too much ingenuity is expended on them. But the cover must be designed to persuade the passer-by to pick it up, whilst the content must be tempting at first glance. At the same time, it should be made quite clear what is offered and what is not, because disappointment through misunderstanding creates bad publicity, and the harm it does can last a long time. Then the demand for the brochure has to be stimulated by press advertisement, television, posters, office display and publicity films – on most evenings from December to April there are scores of promotional film shows up and down the country. The cost of all this is very heavy, and it all has to be budgeted and most of it paid for, before we can know much of what the response is to be. We have to make the best guess out of past experience, and we can still be badly wrong. The market is highly sensitive to influences that cannot be anticipated – the recent sample of arctic weather is a case in point. And the advertisement pages of the popular publications – the

Sunday newspapers in particular — from Christmas to Easter illustrate in a spectacular way the tremendous competition for holiday spending.

So what of the future? The story I have tried to tell covers more than fifty years. Apart from the interruptions of war, and the lesser effect of economic stress, it is a story of constant expansion. Human nature changes, if at all, so slowly as to be almost imperceptible; the 'call of the road' seems to persist as a survival from the dim past when much of mankind was nomadic. So it seems to me likely that in another fifty years time, however vehicles and techniques may evolve, motor-coach tours will still be operating, to more faraway places than ever, giving the same kind of joy they undoubtedly give now — provided we can manage to make the best of our lovely world rather than blow it to bits. Perhaps some of you would like to make a note or observe how my forecast turns out. I may not be here to see.

OMNIBUS SOCIETY PAPERS ON HISTORICAL SUBJECTS

Excluding titles included in the present work or mentioned under Further Reading.

Anon:
Blackpool Corporation Transport. 1956
London in 1910. 1967
Silver Souvenir: Historical Notes on London Transport. 1962

A. Baynton:
Bus Operation in a Holiday Area (East Kent Road Car Company). 1949

J. Graeme Bruce:
Development of Passenger Transport on the Clyde Coast. 1950

D.L. Chalk:
Silent Service: The Story of Bournemouth's Trolley-buses. 1962

J.C. Gillham:
A History of Bolton Corporation Transport. 1948

H.C. Goldspink:
Kingston-upon-Hull Corporation. 1967

R.N. Hannay:
Feathers in their Cap (Guy Motors). 1960

C.T. Humpidge:
The Sheffield Joint Omnibus Committee, its Origins and
   Development. 1963

R.L. Kell (ed):
Sunderland Corporation Transport, a History and Survey.
   1959

J.T. King & A.G. Newman:
Southbound from Croydon. (Published jointly by the OS and
   the Bourne Society).   nd (1964)

C.F. Klapper:
Control of London Passenger Transport. 1932
Organisation of the Omnibus Industry in Great Britain. 1937

A.W. McCall:
Bus and Tram Services from Aldgate to Barking. 1956
London Transport Bus Services in the St Albans Area. nd
   (1960)
Kingsland Road. 1961

T. McLachlan:
Independent Express Services from London to the Coast.
   1959
The Grey-Green Story. 1963

A.J. Mason:
Transport in West Bromwich. 1963

T.B. Maund:
Local Transport in Birkenhead and District. nd (1958)
Transport in Rochdale and District. nd (1959)
Local Transport in Wallasey. 1969
Salford City Transport, a Short History. 1952

L.M.R. Nicholson:
Small Proprietors in the Home Counties. 1931
Limited Stop! Long Distance Coach Services in Great Britain.
1938

L.M.R. Nicholson & C.F. Klapper
Bus Services from London to the Country. Notes on their
Development and Future. 1938

E.N. Osborne:
Ancestry and History of Green Line Coaches. 1953

J.F. Parke:
Devon General. 1966

C.H. Preece:
The History and Development of Express Coach Services.
1958

J.H. Price:
London Buses in Wartime. 1969

C.F. Riley:
Nottingham's Trolleybus System. 1966

N.J.R. Taylor, A.B. James, M.D. Shaw & I.N. Roberts:
City of Oxford, an Illustrated History. 1966

R.H. Truman:
Bus Jubilee. The Growth of West Bridgford UDC Transport
Department. 1965

L.M. Turnham:
The Evolution of the Limited-Stop Coach Services. 1930

The Society also issues, jointly with the PSV Circle, a series of Fleet
Histories of individual companies or groups of operators. In addition to
a wealth of material on acquisition and disposal of vehicles, these papers
include historical notes on the undertakings concerned, and on smaller
businesses that have been acquired.

FURTHER READING

There are two general histories of the motor bus industry — L.A.G. Strong: *The Rolling Road* (Hutchinson, 1956), and John Hibbs: *The History of British Bus Services* (David & Charles, 1968). The evolution of the vehicle has yet to be studied, but a useful list of makers will be found in G.N. Georgano: *The World's Commercial Vehicles* (Temple Press, 1965). On the subjects discussed in the present work, the following books and papers will be found useful:

R.W. **Kidner**: *The London Motor Bus* (Oakwood Press, 1950)

D.L.G. Hunter: *Edinburgh's Transport* (Advertiser Press, Huddersfield, 1964)

J.B. Appleby: *Bristol's Trams Remembered* (published by the author, Westbury-on-Trym, 1969)

J.M. Cummings: *The Rise and Decline of the Railway Bus* (Omnibus Society Paper, 1957)

M. Ginns & E.N. Osborne: *Transport in Jersey* (Transport World, 1961)

K. Hoole: *North Eastern Railway Buses, Lorries and Autocars* (Nidd Valley Narrow Gauge Railways, Knaresborough, 1969)

W. Lambden: *The Manx Transport Systems* (Omnibus Society Paper, 1964)

Charles E. Lee: *The Early Motor Bus* (British Transport Commission, 1962)

On the subject of railway bus services, appropriate mention will usually be found in the standard company histories; further material regarding the GWR services will be found in *Felix J.C. Pole: His Book* (Town & Country Press, Bracknell, 1968) and in G. Behrend: *Gone With Regret* (Jersey Artists, 3rd edn 1969). The subject is also dealt with in the appropriate volumes of David & Charles *Regional History of the Railways of Great Britain.* Individual articles on various aspects of bus and coach history will be found in the pages of *The Omnibus Magazine, The Journal of Transport History* and *Transport History.*

INDEX

Illustrations are indicated by figures in *italic* type. Only principal operators, or those of special significance, are included.

ABC Motor Service (Durham), 64

Aldershot & District Traction Co Ltd, 177

Allen, Thomas & Sons (Blyth), 58-9, 78

Allen, W.P., 195

Alexander, W. & Sons Ltd, 150-1, 176

Allsop, B.J., 166, 126-7, 128

Allsop's Birmingham General Omnibus Co Ltd, 116, 127

Allsopp, E., 141

Anti-Railroad Journal, 147

Appleby, J.B., 8, 208

Associated Daimler Co Ltd, 190

Associated Equipment Co Ltd, 188, 189, 190

Association of London Omnibus Proprietors, 13ff, 21, 32

Axten, E., 10, 94, 95, 116, 124, 159, 160-1, 175

Barnsley & District Traction Co Ltd, 71

Baynton, A., 205

Beatty, Cornelius, 18, 20

Behrend, G., 208

Birch, J.M., 11

Birch, R., 11

Birch, W.H., 23

Birch Bros Ltd, 11ff

Birmingham, 42, 44, *68*, 76, 78, 104, 105, 113ff, *117*, 152, 153, 185 — chart of omnibus proprietors, 116 — control of omnibus operation in, 122-3, 132ff —

early motor bus services, 141ff

Birmingham & Aston Tramways Co Ltd, 116, 124, 127, 140-1

Birmingham & District Omnibus Co Ltd, 116, 129-30

Birmingham & District Tramways Co Ltd, 116, 125

Birmingham & Midland Motor Omnibus Co Ltd ('Midland Red'), 37, 76, 116, 144, 146, 166

Birmingham & Midland Tramways Ltd, *68*, 116, 124, 131, 132, 139-40, 144, 145-6

Birmingham Central Tramways Co Ltd, 116, 124, 128-9, 130, 133

Birmingham Daily Post, 141

Birmingham General Omnibus Co Ltd (1897), 116, 131-2, 134

Birmingham General Omnibus Co Ltd (Allsop's), 116, 127

Birmingham Motor Express Co Ltd, 116, 142, 143-4, 145

Birmingham Omnibus Co, 116, 123

Birmingham Omnibus Conveyance Co, 115, 116, 119, 125, 126

Birmingham Tramways & Omnibus Co Ltd, 116, 126, 128

Booth, G.A., 10, 35

Brandsby, R., 126

Bristol, *68*, 104ff, 110, 111

Bristol Corporation, 106-7, 111

Bristol Omnibus Co Ltd, 8, 104

Bristol Tramways & Carriage Co Ltd, *67*, 104ff, 110ff, 166, 167

Bristol Tramways Co, *67*, 107-8
British Automobile Traction Co Ltd, 102, 187, 189
British Electric Traction Co Ltd, 62, 71, 98ff, 102, 116, 130, 131ff, 137ff, 144, 178, 187ff, 191
Brown, David & Sons Ltd, 185
Brown, F., 185
Bruce, J. Graeme, 54, 205
Bullock, J. & Sons, (1928) Ltd, 70

Calder Bus Co (Brighouse), 90, 92-3
Cannon, A.E., 194
Chalk, D.L., 205
Chaplin, W.J., 148, 149, 152
Chapman, Miss E.M., 138
Chapman, T., 137, 138, 139
Charabancs, 37, 39, 77, 83, 93, 129, 134, 140, 193, 194
City of Birmingham Tramways Co Ltd, 116, 131, 137, 139, 140, 142, 144-5
City Omnibus Co Ltd, 13
Clan Motorways (Glasgow), 76
Clarkson, T., 183
Coast Line (Edinburgh), 58
Continental tours, 195ff
Coras Iompair Eireann, 45, 180
Cornwall Motor Transport Co Ltd, 165
Cornwall Omnibus Co (London), 15
Cort, R., 147
Cox, R., 52
Crossley, Firth, 83
Crosville Motor Co Ltd, 165, 177
Cummings, J.M., 179, 208

Daimler-BSA group of companies, 183, 184, 185, 190
Daimler Motor Co (1904) Ltd, 184, 185, 186ff
Darlington Triumph Services, 8, 64, 65
Devon General Omnibus & Tour-

ing Co Ltd, 165-6, 207
Devon Motor Transport Co Ltd, 165
Doughty, J., 113, 114
Dravers, W.M., 103
Durham, *50*, 63, 64, 74, 79
Durham District Services Ltd, 65

Eastbourne, early coach tour from, 193
Eastern Counties Omnibus Co Ltd, 60
Eastern Counties Road Car Co Ltd, 174
Eastern National Omnibus Co Ltd, 174
Eastern Scottish, fleet name, 56
East Midland Motor Services Ltd, 77, 79
East Kent Road Car Co Ltd, 205
East Yorkshire Motor Services Ltd, 77, 80, 173
Edgbaston Omnibus Co Ltd (Birmingham), 116, 126
Edinburgh, 34ff, *49*, 54, 55ff, 72ff, 79, 153
Edinburgh Autocar Co, 36
Edinburgh & District Tramways Co, 35, 37, 57
Edinburgh Northern Cable Tramways Co, 35
Edinburgh Street Tramway Co, 35
Erdington Omnibus Department (Birmingham), 141n
European Economic Community, 200n
Evans, Rev J., 105
Eve, Sir Tristram, 164
Extended tours, 192ff, 197-8, 203

Farndale, J., 101
Fawdon Bus Co Ltd, 78
Fooks-Bale, J.H., 182
Fraser, Capt Ian, MP, 19
Frost-Smith, P., 185, 186

Gailey, T.W.H., 104

Galleys Express Motors (Newcastle-upon-Tyne), 80
Gateshead & District Tramways Co Ltd, 62
Gearless Motor Omnibus Co Ltd, 184, 189
General County Omnibus Co Ltd, 54, 63
General Tramways Co Ltd (Birmingham), 125
Georgano, G.N., 208
Gillham, J.C., 205
Ginns, M., 208
Glenton Friars (Road Coaches) Ltd, 72-3
Goldspink, H.C., 205
Gray, I.L., 103
Great North of England Omnibus Co, 78
Greener, W.W., 141

Hackney Carriages, 105, 106, 122, 133
Halifax, 50, 82, 84ff, 180
Halifax Joint Committee, 95-6, 180
Hall, J. & E., Ltd, 185
Hannay, R.N., 206
Hanson, Joseph & Sons, Ltd, 102
Harrogate Carriage Co, 84
Harrogate Road Car Co Ltd, 66, 84
Hebble Motor Services Ltd, 50, 81ff, 94ff, 98ff
Hilton, C.B.S., 144
Holdsworth, O. & C., 82, 84, 92ff
Hoole, K., 208
Horne, B.W., 148, 149, 152, 153
Horse buses, 11, 34, 106, 111-12, 113ff, 148ff
Horse trams, 35, 37, 67, 108-9, 125ff
Huddersfield, 84, 86ff, 90, 92ff, 96, 180
Humpidge, C.T., 206
Hunter, D.L.G., 208

Iden, W.J., 184
Illustrated Morning News (Birmingham), 117
Independent proprietors: impact of London Traffic Act, 1924 on, 13ff, 18ff − in Birmingham, 114ff − in London, 11ff, 20, 155

Jackson, Sir Henry, MP, 16, 19
James, A.B., 207
James, J. & Sons, Ltd (Ammanford), 166
Jenson, A.G., 113, 116, 124

Keighley-West Yorkshire Services Ltd, 66, 69
Kell, R.L., 205
Kidner, R.W., 208
King, J.T., 205
Klapper, C.F., 206, 207

Lambden, W., 208
Lancashire United Transport & Power Ltd, 78
Lee, C.E., 147, 179, 181, 193, 208
Leeds, 13, 77ff, 88-9, 94-5, 99, 101, 104
Leeds & Newcastle Omnibus Co Ltd, 78
Licensing, 13, 83, 85ff, 88, 89, 92, 122-3, 132, 138, 142
Limited Stop Pool, the, 77ff
Lincolnshire Road Car Co Ltd, 60
Little, W.M., 42, 48, 51
London, 11ff, 36, 54, 55, 58, 72ff, 98, 105-6, 133, 135, 136, 149, 181ff, 194, 206-7 − railway stations, 12, 13, 149, 153ff, 172, 187 − traffic pool, 186, 189
London & District Motorbus Co Ltd, 181
London & Home Counties Traffic Advisory Committee, 14ff, 22, 29

London & South Coast Motor Services Ltd, 195
London & Suburban Traction Co Ltd, 188-9
London Coastal Coaches Ltd, 74, 76
London County Council, 155
London General Country Services Ltd, 167, 171
London General Omnibus Co Ltd, 12, 19, 20, 23, 25, 26, 28, 29, 33, *135, 136,* 166, 170-1, 181ff
London, Midland & Yorkshire Services Ltd, 77
London Public Omnibus Co Ltd, 20, 23, 25
London Transport, 8, 44, 54, 167, 205, 206
London United Tramways Ltd, 188
Long distance services, 71ff, 93, 99, 101-2, 207
Lycett, J.A., 144

McCall, A.W., 206
Mackenzie, A.D., 194
Mackenzie, W., 130
McLachlan, T., 206
MacShanes Motors Ltd (Liverpool), 79
Maidstone & District Motors Services Ltd, 103
Majestic Saloon Coaches (London & Newcastle) Ltd, 72, 73
Manville, E., 184, 189
Mason, A.J., 206
Mathews, W., 105, 106
Mathews' New History of Bristol, 104
Maund, T.B., 206
Metropolitan Electric Tramways Ltd, 187ff
Midland Bus Services Ltd, 76
Midland Omnibus Co (Birmingham), 115, 116, 119, 120
Montreal Tramways Co, 130
Motorways Ltd, 195

Musselburgh & District Electric Light & Traction Co Ltd, 36, 58

Nairn, A., 34
National Electric Construction Co Ltd, 58
National Bus Company, 104, 178
National Omnibus & Transport Co Ltd, 167, 171
National Steam Car Co Ltd, 174
Nevin & District Motor Omnibus Co Ltd, 168
Newcastle-upon-Tyne, 52, 54, 55, 58, 60, 61-2, 72ff, 77ff − toll on High Level Bridge at, 61
Newington Motor & Engineering Co Ltd (Hull), 174
Newman, A.G., 205
Newnes, Sir George, 158
Nicholson, L.M.R., 207
Northern General Transport Co Ltd, 54, 61, 62-3, 77, 78
North Western Road Car Co Ltd, 77

OK Motor Services (Bishop Auckland), 65
Omnibuses, 113ff, 148ff
Orange Bros Ltd, 71, 74
Osborne, E.N., 207, 208
Overground Ltd, 12
Overland Motor Services, 79
Oxford, City of, Motor Services Ltd, 45

Parke, J.F., 207
Phillips, E.M., 22
Phillipson Stella Motor Services Ltd, 54, 74
Pick, F., 12, 32, 183
Pilcher, R. Stuart, 37
Pity Me, 63, 73
Pointon, F.K., 103
Pole, Sir Felix, J.C., 161, 208

Police, Chief Constables of, Birmingham, 132, 134, 142 — London, 15, 16, 19
Police, Commissioner of, London, 12, 23ff, 27-8
Potteries Motor Traction Co Ltd, 53
Power, O.C., 140, 145
Preece, C.H., 207
Premier Motorbus Co Ltd, 183, 185-6
Price, J.H., 207
Pudney, J., 190n

Railway Gazette, 8
Railway companies: Alexandra (Newport & South Wales), 157, 179 — Caledonian, 169, 179 — Cambrian, 157, 169 — Glasgow & South Western, 169, 179 — Great Eastern, 158, 173-4, 175, 179 — Great Northern, 172, 179 — Great North of Scotland, 158, 159, 174, 176, 179 — Great Western, 149, 156-7, 158, 162ff, 173, 179 — London & North Eastern, 60, 63, 71, 75, 79, 150, 158, 173ff, 177, 178, 179 — London & North Western, 157, 169ff, 179 — London & South Western, 149, 153, 167, 179 — London Midland & Scottish, 71, 100, 157, 177-8, 179 — Lynton & Barnstaple, 158-9 — Metropolitan, 154-5, 179 — Midland, 168, 169, 172ff, 179 — Newcastle & Berwick, 153 — North British, 153, 179 — North Eastern, 63, 158, 173, 179, 208 — North Staffordshire, 157, 179
Railway companies' road powers, 157ff, 165, 177
Redwing Safety Services Ltd, 79
Restricted Street Orders, 13ff, 16ff, 21
Ribble Motor Services Ltd, 101, 102

Roberts, I.N., 207
Rossdale, P.M., 98
Ross, J., 130, 131

SB&S Syndicate, 185-6
Scotland Yard, 133, 170 — Public Carriage Office, 22, 133
Scottish Bus Group, 51
Scottish General (Northern) Omnibus Co Ltd, 176
Scottish Motor Traction Co Ltd, 37, 55ff, 72, 74-6, 176, 178
Scottish Omnibuses Ltd, 55-6
Searle, Colonel Frank, 135, 181ff
Shaw, M.P., 207
Sheffield Joint Omnibus Committee, 205
Sheffield United Tours Ltd, 103
Shillibeer, George, 113
Southdown Motor Services Ltd, 193
Southern National Omnibus Co Ltd, 168
South Metropolitan Electric Tramways & Lighting Co Ltd, 188, 189
South Staffs & Birmingham District Steam Tramways Ltd, 124
South Wales Transport Co Ltd, 103
South Yorkshire Motors Ltd, 70
Spencer, H.J., 195
Standerwick, E.V., 194
Stanley, Alfred (later Lord Ashfield), 187
Stanley & Wasbrough, Messrs, 106-7
Starbuck Car Co, 108
Steam buses, 34, 173 — Clarkson (make of), 66, 176, 182-3
Steam wagons, 82, 93
Stevens, W.A., 185
Subsidies, paid by railway companies for bus services, 149, 156, 162, 180
Sword, J.C., 76

Taylor, E.L., 9, 191
Taylor, N.J.R., 207
Tebbitt, C., 116, 130
Thackray, R., 20
Thames Valley Traction Co Ltd,
  167
Thomson, R.W., 34
Tilling, Richard S., 185
Tilling & British Automobile Trac-
  tion Co Ltd, 60, 74, 177
Tilling, Thomas, Ltd, 11, 74, 94,
  156, 178, 185ff
Tobutt, J.W., 132
Tocia Motor Omnibus Co (North
  Wales), 160
Tolerton, R.H., 87
Traffic Commissioners, 74, 80,
  102 — Metropolitan area, 27 —
  Northern area, 72   — North
  Western area, 101
Train, George Francis, 125
Tramway & Railway World, 131
Tramways (MET) Omnibus Co
  Ltd, 187, 188
Transport History, 208
Transport History, Journal of, 208
Transport, Minister of; Ministry
  of, 13ff, 55
Trolleybuses, 61, 62, 65, 69, 71
Truman, R.H., 207
Turnham, L.M., 207
Tyne, river, 61, 153

Ulster Transport Authority, 180
Underground Electric Railways Co
  of London Ltd, 189
Underground group of companies,
  12, 187, 188
Underwood Express Services Ltd,
  77
United Automobile Co Ltd, 58,
  59-60, 61, 63ff, 72ff, 78-9 ,
  173-4
United Motor Omnibus Co Ltd,
  13

Vanguard Motor Omnibus Co Ltd,
182, 183
Vehicles, chassis for:
  ADC, 190; 423, 39 — AEC,
  188, 189; 403, 37; 507, 39 —
  Bridgemaster, 47, 48; Q-type,
  40; Regal, *50*, 196; Regent, 42,
  45; Reliance, 39, 40, 46, *118;*
  Renown, 52; Y-type, 37 — Albion, 89, 100, 169; Aberdonian,
  46; Lowlander, 52; PMB 28,
  39, 40; Viking, 88 — Bedford,
  199; OB, 42; SB5, 51, 52; SB8,
  46;   VAL1, 51; VAL14, 52;
  VAS1, 51, 52 — Berliet, 196 —
  Bristol; K5G, 42; L5G, 42 —
  Commercar, 172 — Crossley:
  Alpha, 39, 40; Bridgemaster,
  45; SD42, 42; — Daimler, 36,
  40, 41, 59, 72-3, 86, 170, 172,
  184, 187-9; CC, 194; CF6, 39,
  40; CH6, 39; CLG5, 45; COG5,
  40, 42; COT4, 40; CP6, 39;
  CVD6, 42; CVG5, 42; CVG6,
  42, 47; Fleetline, 52; Freeline,
  43; KPL, 185 — de Dion, 182,
  183, 186 — Dennis, 21, 39,
  193ff; E-type, 92; Loline, 47
  — Durkopp, 143ff — Ford, R226,
  52 — Gilford, 72 — Gotfredson,
  92 — GER, 174 — Guy, 43, 47
  75, 206; Arab, 42, 44, 45; FBB,
  118; Wulfrunian, 48 — Halford-
  Stevens, 185 — Karrier, 194;
  WL6, 39 — Lacoste-Battman,
  181 — Leyland, 37, 54, 59,
  86, 88, 169-70, 172; Atlantean,
  48, 52; LB5, 11; Leopard, 48,
  49, 51; PD2, 44, 47; PLSC
  Lion, 39, 40, 88, 92, 171; RAF-
  type, 83; Royal Tiger, 43, 47,
  51; TD7, 42, 44; Tiger, 97, 196;
  Tiger Cub, 43, 46, 47, 48; Titan,
  45, 51 — Leyland/MCW: HR40
  Olympic, 43, 48 — LGOC, 181ff;
  B-type, *135*, *136*, 183, 189;
  X-type, *135*, 183 — Lothian,
  56 — Maudslay, 55, 56, 172 —

Milnes-Daimler, 143ff, 158, 163-4, 168, 170ff, 176 — Morris Imperial, 39, *49* — Morris Commercial Dictator, 39 — Mulliner, 142-3 — Saurer, 177, 196 — Sentinel, 43 — Stirling, 36 — Straker-Squire, 62 — Thornycroft, 143, 145, 169, 172, 176-7 — Tilling-Stevens, 37, 42 — Tyrgan, 181 — Wolseley, 143, 145, 172, 183

Vehicles, engines for:
AEC, 40 — Beardmore, 40 — Commer TS3, 45 — Crossley, 40 — Gardner, 40, 45 — Knight, 56 — Leyland, 44, 46 — Mercedes, 171 — Napier, 143 — Tangye, 40 — Thornycroft, 40

Vehicles, makes of body for:
Alexander, 39, 43, 45ff, 48, 53 — Barnaby, 89 — Beadle, 45, 53 — Birch, 11 — Bristol, 42 — Brush, 37, 39, 43, 53 — Crossley, 45, 53 — Duple, 43, 44, 46, 53 — Eastern Counties, 97 — English Electric, 39 — Fielding & Bottomley, 89 — Fry, 37 — Guy, 53 — Hall Lewis, 97 — Hora, 37 — Hume, 39 — Leyland, 83 — Massey Bros, 89 — MCW, 44, 45, 47, 53 — Metropolitan Cammell, 39, 40, 41, 45 — Northern Coachbuilders, 53 — Northern Counties, 42 — Pickering, 47 — Plaxton, 53 — Roe, 53 — Roberts, 40 — Saro, 43, 53 — Sentinel, 43, 53 — Snapes, 89 — Vickers, *118* — Weymann, 40, 43, 46, 48 — Willowbrook, 42, 47, 53

Wallace Arnold Tours, 102
War Transport, Ministry of, 42
Western National Omnibus Co Ltd, 167
Western SMT Co Ltd, 52, 76
West London Association, 17ff
West Riding Automobile Co Ltd, 69-70
West Yorkshire Road Car Co Ltd, 66ff, 76ff, 80, 101-2
White, A.J., 103
Wibsey Flyer, the, 102
Wills, J.S., 98-9
Wilson, R.P., 140
Winchester, Marquis of, 23
Wolseley Tool & Motor Co Ltd, 143
Wolsey, Walter, Jnr, 84, 185
Wolverhampton, 114, 115, 131, 167
Wreathall, C.R.H., 103

Yorkshire Pool, the, 76ff
Yorkshire Traction Co Ltd, 69, 70-71, 76, 81, 101, 102
Yorkshire Woollen District Transport Co Ltd, 76, 77, 84, 94, 101, 102
Yorkshire (West Riding) Electric Tramways Co Ltd, 69